For Mary,
my sweet faithful
friend
Jull

SHERDS

a Mémoire

By

Jule Moon

Sherds

a Mémoire

Copyrighted
By
Jule Moon

ISBN number: 978-1463565497

Original Printings

Reprints of poems and articles from the original or first printing –

I list the following:
  Jule Moon, Water Memories, What is the Color of a
  Hurricane, Something to like About a Storm, A
  House Speaks, Laddie's Ivan Adventure first ap-
  peared in *Writing Mobile Bay,* the *Hurricane
  Project,* printed by the Alabama Writers' Forum,
  Inc. and funded by the Forum and the Alabama
  State Council on the Arts, 2006.

  Jule Moon, August 1966 first appeared in the *Alcalde*, Austin, Texas,
1986.
  Jule Moon, Displaced Thinking Can Lead to Violence, first appeared
in the *Mobile Register,* October 4, 2006.

TABLE OF CONTENTS

Sherds – a Mémoire

Foreword

By

Suzanne Hudson and Joe Formichella

What a great lady. Jule Moon. Hers is certainly a name befitting an author, lyrical, like the seed of a poem. It's a name that coaxes symbolic layers from its strand of letters. It's a name that speaks a sparkling existence.

Jule—a jewel, which, after an exhilarating life of learned lessons—some harsh but ultimately uplifting—is a woman revealed in a multifaceted sparkle that is her smile. Even as she approaches a century's worth of living, that smile of hers is as youthful as it ever was.

Moon—a life force, a mover—of tides, of rhythms, of spirits. She is a constant and eager consumer of ideas, thoughts, ways of looking at the world that make her a magnet for good, intelligent people who are drawn to her shimmering, enviable energy. It is a thing she surely must have felt early but could not identify, as a young girl welcoming to everyone and everything, unafraid where others feared to veer from the mundane, the feebly anemic status quo. Surely she somehow already knew that listening and laughter bind us all in every way. And now, here, fortunately, she's allowing us to listen and laugh along with her.

Within these pages she shares her memories of growing up in Mobile, Alabama; her steadfast affinity to family; her unique experiences as a "career woman" (and a serial one at that, growing through several professional incarnations) before that was so fashionable for a "proper lady" in the South; her loves and her losses; and her strength of spirit that is so inspiring to those of us who hunger for such nourishment in our own existences.

And she is offering it to us. She has collected up the sherds of her experiences and fixed them together into these reminiscences, stories, and poems for the rest of us to enjoy. And while we're at it, if we keep our hearts open, at the ready, we might just catch some of the spiritual glitter that is the soul of, yes, a truly, truly great lady.

Preface

I made a connection between poetry and music very early in my childhood. I view poetry as an imaginative, artful, rhythmic reflection of an emotional experience containing a contrasting or unexpected ending and communicated clearly and pictorially to the reader. The words and rhyme chosen should constitute a meaningful fit. As in every artistic expression, I believe the style and content chosen by the poet is a reflection of the culture of the times and of the personality of the writer but should contain a timeless universality.

My discovery in the study of archeology at the University of Texas when I was eighteen that a small incomplete collection of sherds, broken remnants of clay, could offer a view into the habits, beliefs and character of a people; my exploration in the field of paleontology which illustrates that casts of extinct sea creatures found in limestone deposited millions of years ago could provide an index to the time and circumstances of their demise and thus reveal a location useful in the work of geologists searching for petroleum; my thirty years of psychiatric practice using principles of Gestalt psychology which propounds that individuals exhibit essential patterns of behavior and that this diagnostic information can enable treatment professionals to understand the character and tendencies of persons and thereby assist them in changing their lives – all these concepts and experiences in my three professions coalesced in an idea which prompted the title and the presentation of this memoire.

The poems and vignettes take their structure from the various musical, dramatic, and artistic involvements in my youth which I chose to add color, variety, and excitement to my life.

The resulting writings are the sherds of my existence, not the whole story nor even a resume, but I hope they are sufficient to convey the essence of my history, my philosophy of living, and my life's work.

Jule Marion Jacobson Moon

Introduction

I was influenced by my parents' talents for storytelling, their knowledge, kindness, tolerance, and humor; and the encouragement of my grade school and high school teachers, and I suppose because a third grade teacher asked me to write a poem about Christmas.

I was led to poetry by the love of the beauty and emotionality of music, the musicality and the art of poetry, the morality of the nursery rhymes, the fantasy of the fairy tales, the universality of Aesop's Fables, the mystery and majesty of the Bible; the glory of the drama; the magic of language; the terseness and realism of journalism; the discovery and romance of archeology and geology; the essence of Gestalt psychology, the humanism and insight of nursing, psychiatry and social work. The pictorial, dramatic life lessons of the early motion pictures and the style and treatment of subject matter by O. Henry influenced my choice of the short story, and Edgar Allen Poe, Emily Dickenson and nearly all of the 17th, 19th and 20th century poets inspired me to use poetry as well to convey my life history.

All these are in me and in my memoire, the title of which is Sherds, an archeological term meaning preserved fragments from which can be derived the story of the life of a people.

Acknowledgments

I am indebted to the persons represented here in these stories and poems for their influence on many of the choices I have made in my life. This Memoire is a tribute to them. The names and locales of some of the individuals have been changed to respect their privacy.

The idea for the Memoire began in 2007 after the completion of the anthology, **Writing Mobile Bay: The Hurricane Project**, printed by the Alabama Writers' Forum, Inc. and funded by the Forum and the Alabama State Council on the Arts. My thanks to Jeanie Thompson, executive director of the Alabama Writers' Forum, Inc., for her constant encouragement during the writing of the Hurricane Project.

Following the completion of the Project several writers in the community, led by a teaching staff including the Project's teachers, Roy Hoffman, Suzanne Hudson, and Joe Formichella, conducted a series of classes covering their orientation to fiction writing. Other authors in the community were invited, including Terry Cline, Judith Richards, and Sonny Brewer. Many thanks to them for their interest, support and guidance.

Following these meetings, the Fairhope Writers' Group was formed out of the writers who continued to meet regularly as a group dedicated to the serious pursuit of improving their craft and setting goals. These members are Ron Meszaros, Roger Bull, Karen Bull, Mary Ardis, Beth Knox, Bob Glennon, Ken James, Vicki Armitage and myself.

Special thanks to Ron Meszaros for his expert critiquing, suggestions and guidance; to Mary Ardis for her expert typing and to Roger Bull for his expertise and hours of work on the formatting. Thanks to Katherine Thompson for her diligent assistance with the proof.

Without their continuous encouragement, support, and valuable critiquing of my work, this book would be a collection of miscellaneous memory sketches in the bottom of a drawer.

Legacy

I am Georgia, Alabama, Oklahoma, and Texas
You have owned me, nurtured me and branded me
And I am your indentured child

I feel the soft cloak of the colors of your climates
I have been chastened and strengthened
by the thrusts of your waves and your windstorms

Your people your legends and your anthems
invade my enterprises
I hear your voices with every day's beginning

When tempted with thoughts of surrender or despair
I hear your stern reproach, your gentle urgings
Turn away start again look up.

Chapter 1 – Mothers of Mobile

All the children were crying. They were leaning out of the windows reaching backward and straining to see Linda waving from the front yard. Daddy's big dark blue Buick was taking them away from their beloved Georgia. Georgia of the red clay hills, the dark green Junipers and the red brick houses. And the grey Stone Mountain they could see from their breakfast room windows.

It was 1932, a bad year in America and a bad year in Atlanta. Julie heard her parents talking about "the depression." The children did not think it was bad at all. They lived in a big red brick house with white trim and trees all around. Lee and Frank had a large room big enough for friends to come and play in. Of course they shared it with Granddaddy. It was there he showed them how to build all sorts of things with their Erector Set while he told them grand stories of the old country.

Julie had her own room too with lacy wallpaper blooming with lavender pansy faces. She wondered if the new house would have a room for her with flower faces. She would always see the flower faces. From her window at night she could look out and see the brilliant lights of the Sears and Roebuck Co. sign blinking on and off atop the store miles away.

As if the room were not enough, Granddaddy built a whole new house for her. She had wished for a dollhouse, a small one like the one belonging to her friend Betty. But Granddaddy always did things in the grand manner. He insisted on building a little house like Mama's with a porch and railings and all. Julie was trying to see the grey roof of the little house now.

Miss Christina stepped out in front of the group of neighbors who had awakened at 5 A.M. to wave goodbye to the children. She was the one who prayed beside Julie's bed that night when the doctors thought she would die. Julie thought for a moment about the long illness of bronchial asthma and the long confinement in her room when her only companions were her books.

Now the children were straining to glean the last sight of Linda who was remaining behind. Linda was crying too and holding in her white apron the pictures of the children that were the only parting gifts she requested when Mama told her to take what she wanted of the furniture and ornaments being left behind. She especially wanted the framed one of Frank, her "baby."

Linda was a tall, thin, light skinned young Negro woman, in her early 20s. She was a perfect lady. She spoke in a sweet low voice. She was always neat and her manners were a model for the children. She wore elbow length sleeves and plain colors. On company for dinner days or holidays she wore a long sleeved black uniform, a short white scalloped apron and a headdress Julie thought of as a white starched tiara. She was always very proper, even formal.

She had Thursdays off, the usual day for servants in Atlanta, and then it became Granddaddy's time to take the children somewhere for a treat, usually the Grand picture show downtown. But still they missed Linda and greeted her on Friday as if she had been gone a long time. "We missed you, Linda," they would clamor, dancing all around her, and they would tell her all about the day on Thursday or about the picture show.

There would never be another Linda. They would miss her all their lives.

Mama was one of those modern women. She never bobbed her hair, never had it curled or marcelled, the current fashion, and she did not have a career. But she thought of herself as "specializing in the cooking, supervising the housekeeping" and came into her own at the bridge table. She played mah jong too, but Mama was something to reckon with at afternoon bridge. She would often refer to it as her "old age insurance." She was ahead of her time in realizing the value of a hobby as necessary to keeping one's mind alert and involved in old age.

The bulk of the housekeeping and child tending was Linda's domain, as was the custom at that time among many Southern families. Linda said she was losing "her family." Although in the thirties the title of "nurse" had long replaced "mammy," to the children she would always be "second Mama."

"I'm going to name my little girl for you, Linda," Julie was calling.

"Me, too," thought Frank.

Lee was crying too, but he was crying also for Granddaddy who had gone ahead and was staying temporarily with Uncle Frank in Texas until the family got settled in Mobile. Lee was the older of the two brothers, tall and slender and athletically inclined, playing golf like Daddy. Frank looked like Buster Brown with his haircut and short pants. He was the one who would accompany Julie on neighborhood walks, saying very little but listening intently to his sister.

"How long until we get to the new house, Daddy?" Julie asked.

She was the traveler, already having spent several summers with Great Aunt Minnie in Daddy's childhood home in Camden, South Carolina. Therefore she began to think ahead to the house of the future as well as the one of the past. That's the blessing of travelers, she guessed, they learn to leave and say goodbye to their home. (Granddaddy always referred to her as "the philosopher.")

"How long, Daddy?"

"Late tonight, Daughter."

"The street you said we'd be living on has a funny name," complained Lee. "I like Linwood better."

"Bienville is a French name, Son. Mobile was settled by the French, Georgia by the English. So there will be many French names to learn."

Mama was fond of saying that Daddy should have been a professor. Daddy believed everyone should know history. A person wasn't educated if he didn't know history. Mama agreed the children needed to know the history of the whole world, even Asia.

"Alabama is a very good place to learn history, children." As he drove Daddy would point out a monument or historical landmark, occasionally stopping to read it aloud.

"Look," he said, "at the great stand of southern pines ahead."

"How beautiful," said Mama. She loved to garden, and she especially loved trees, having planted many varieties of fruit trees in Atlanta.

"They are the ones pulp paper is made from," said Daddy. "That's the business of the Paper Mill where my office will be."

It was late in the afternoon. The children began crying again. Daddy became impatient. They were in Alabama now and there was much to see and he wanted them to be observant.

"Will there be a Cyclorama with the history of the Civil War?" Julie asked excitedly. "No mountains?"

"No, but there is Dog River and Mobile Bay and the Gulf of Mexico a few miles away. And Mardi Gras! You'll have many surprises in store for you."

The children became quiet.

"You must remember," Mama said softly, "the children are after all leaving their motherland."

"These children are lucky," Daddy said sternly. They have a beautiful scenic place to go to, parents who care for them, and I have a new position at the new Paper Mill. As I see it they will have a new motherland."

Mama raised her eyebrows inquiringly, "I didn't know there could be but one motherland."

Daddy conceded, "All right then."

Mama was always pleased with herself when she could offer an idea to match Daddy's, "One motherland in a lifetime but maybe there will be mothering people to tend and teach and be kind to the children like the ones we knew in Atlanta."

The children listened in spite of their tears. They liked to hear their parents discussing them in the way of telling a story. The way it was done was comforting.

It was dark when they arrived at Bienville Avenue. In the moonlight they could see the green trimmed grey stucco two-story house. The yard was covered with azaleas and Japonicas. A giant live oak tree in the front yard shaded the house. A tall magnolia reached to the balcony on the second story. A giant Poinsettia as high as the house was on the other side. Julie learned the balcony was outside of her bedroom. Her own balcony!

The screened front porch contained a glider and other porch furniture. Mama said it was wrought iron. The first look at their new home was a pleasant surprise. The children awakened in the morning on quilts and comforters on the hardwood floor of the living room. The furniture would be arriving by midday. The horse drawn farmer's wagon was heard rumbling down the street. The doorbell was ringing. A tall elegant gray-haired lady was smiling and extending a generous sized pan of homemade hot rolls and butter. Beside her was a pretty brown haired 13-year-old girl.

"Welcome to Bienville Avenue," said Miss Ida. "And this is my daughter, Mary."

Miss Ida, who lived directly across the street, was obviously a leader in the neighborhood, Julie observed. Hot rolls for breakfast were a new treat. Mama had preferred rye bread and assorted rolls from the bakery. She was delighted to learn from Miss Ida that Smith's Bakery on Dauphin Street was a favorite of all in the neighborhood.

Miss Jimmie next door would arrive next with what would become known as her famous Crisco coconut cake. Miss Jimmie was sweet looking and plump and you could tell never one to be upset over anything.

The fashionable Miss Winona in her Jumonville designed dress (a French couturier recently moved to Mobile), who worked at the First National Bank, left her card on her way to work. She said her son Arch was studying to be an architect. He was away now but would call later. Her mother, Miss Catherine, obviously the matriarch of the community, came to call and stayed the rest of the morning. She discussed the small new neighborhood grocery called Delchamps a few blocks away. Miss Catherine was giving it the French pronunciation. Julie's eyes widened at her first French lesson. Miss Catherine also recommended the larger A and P grocery farther up on Dauphin Street.

"More French," said Julie.

From next door on the left came Helen, a smartly dressed young woman up and coming in the business world, a furniture buyer. Julie was thrilled to hear her say there were several more girls and boys her age farther up the street.

Dr. McVay lived around the corner on Dauphin Street. His driveway extended back opposite Julie's upstairs room. His black Packard coming and going at all hours of the night and early morning was the beginning of her realization of the meaning of devotion necessary for one in the healing profession.

Down the street toward Murphy High School were more mothers. Miss Cornelia coached math, fortunately as it would turn out for Julie. Miss Nina would advise Mama on the culture of azaleas and would share her knowledge of persimmons whose examples were the envy of the neighborhood. The ladies commented on the large Satsuma and the fig trees in the back yard. Mama was immediately at home in this lush environment.

By afternoon the furniture arrived, as well as the neighborhood children turned out of school on the last day before summer vacation. They visited on the screened porch while Mama served lemonade and tomato and homemade mayonnaise sandwiches.

It was like a party thought Julie – mothers bringing their many flavored offerings and the children talking excitedly about the occasions of the summer just beginning around and over the Bay. The festive atmosphere was to remain in the neighborhood throughout the era of the Thirties.

So this must be what Daddy meant when he told us Mobile would be a "new motherland," Julie reflected. And Mama said, oh, yes, what was it – that there would be "mothering people."

This then was Bienville Avenue, Mobile, 1932, the place and time of a welcoming the kind the children would never see again. It must have been a mystical place to seem so festive during those years people called the "dark days of the Depression," when strangers transformed themselves into family.

Clockwise: Frank, Jule and Lee Jacobson

Why Poetry

I fell in love with iambic pentameter
enthralled by the lilt of the English tongue
reaching for words that ring with rhythm
words when I'm stalled that move me along

words with a flair for leaves and flowers
winds and birds and all that fly
all that run and dance and flicker
words with power to lift me high

words with muster to hold me steady
words that ply magic to smooth my way
all of the words that soar and sing
and carry me back to that singingest day

The Healer

She was called to this healing early-
the young ones their eyes looking not seeing
their mouths fearful not speaking
their little shoulders untimely stooped
their arms sagging holding nothing
pulling her to them from where they sat
always in a corner always alone.
the girls in their colorless dresses
the boys in old overalls like their fathers
her empathy destined always to be confused with love.

Before them there were the outriders,
the nurses, reaching out with warm smiles and hands
their white authoritative uniforms comforting
reminding her of her Mother's divinity candy,
the physicians who sat by her bedside
for a long time as they did in those days,
the physicians who fathered her recovery
and trained her as they saved her.

In loving memory, Dr. Leon McVay, Sr. of Mobile

Chapter 2 – George

George and I had that lucky kind of boy and girl friendship based on admiration, sharing insights, laughing and working together. It was the kind of open happy relationship I took for granted and expected would exist with the men in my adult life. I didn't know then that ours was a relationship of special equality.

There were other boys back then in that other kind of not so equal relationship in which the boy did the choosing, the asking and paying for the privilege, while the girl had only to worry about measuring up to some unspoken and unknown contract.

The other boys were Leo, who often walked home with me and carried my books, sometimes sitting on our porch and sharing a cool lemonade, Leon and Jack who escorted me to a fancy party now and then, Richard who called in advance for real dates to the movies down town, and Victor who could be counted on to select the ice cream parlor on a warm summer evening. I cannot remember anything any of them ever said to me.

George and I met in journalism class, an elective for junior students with certain credits in English. He turned around from his seat in front of me and introduced himself, "I'm George, and I know who you are, you played the lead in the Four Arts Club play last year and you sing in the trio in the Glee Club." George was of medium height and with dark eyes and hair. His parents were of Spanish and English ancestry (It was a southern custom to discuss family heritage in the first conversation). His engaging smile and openness promised a good-humored disposition. Some considered him shy, but he was never shy with me.

George and I became partners in an exciting adventure, a small part of a larger world, the world of journalism. There was a bond between us that insured support for any eventuality that suggested even a small threat.

Our niche was the journalism class, and the after school activities required work on a varied and large number of tasks involved in publishing the Murphy Hi Times, the weekly newspaper.

George was a clever feature writer, his good humor and sincerity apparent in his writing. I enjoyed the challenge of the duties as makeup editor and headline writer. I occasionally wrote a poem for the poet's column. If there were ever a dispute about the paper's makeup, or a questionable headline, or how much protest we might be allowed in an argument with the faculty (I recall my request to interview inmates in the County Jail) George was always on my side. I seem to remember he carried more weight than I did.

Our junior year ended and preparations were made for the election of class officers and the Editor of the Hi Times. The members of the journalism class who worked on the paper would continue their jobs after class in the senior year. Campaign managers would be in charge of the campaign, making and distributing posters in the halls and making speeches in the auditorium. I was the campaign manager for my friend Mary who was running for president of the senior class. She campaigned for me as editor. George was also nominated for that position.

He protested from the beginning that he preferred writing features. There had to be two candidates and no one else wanted the responsibility. I knew the title wouldn't make any difference because my job would be the same, except for some additional oversight and decision-making. The teacher called me aside a few days before the election and told me she wanted me to be the editor. I was shocked and disappointed at her actions and thought she was being unfair. I told George and he said, "Never mind, you know I never wanted the position anyway." The results were posted and I lost. I was disappointed, but I knew that George was better known, having lived in Mobile all his life, and I was a newcomer from Atlanta three years before.

My parents had already prepared me several times before for the possibility of losing a contest. My Father, frequently cautioned me, referring to the game of poker, "it may appear that you have a winning hand and you can still lose." This good advice was usually followed by the familiar reference to the Battle of Camden in the Revolutionary war (he was a native of Camden, South Carolina) in which "the defenders relied on their territorial advantage, but were surprised in combat, outmanned and outgunned." I had learned these lessons well, and in later years they served to save me a lot of unnecessary stress and enabled me to attribute equal weight to luck and skill in just about any competition.

The next day George resigned. He found out from some of the students that the teacher had told her classes to vote for him. He only said to me "You know I never wanted the job in the first place."

I was moved up to the position of editor. However I was still puzzled by the fact that the teacher had said one thing to me and another to the students. The authority of teachers had always been important to me and I felt shaken. George waited after school that day to walk home with me.

"You know," he said, talking more slowly than usual, "teachers sometimes get mixed up when they try to please everybody." That certainly fit our teacher! George knew people all right, a characteristic guaranteed to make him a good feature writer.

It was George who reminded me of all she had done for us earlier in the year, in fact just a few months ago. She arranged for seven students to accompany her to an international association convention for journalism students to be held at Columbia University in New York. Among the speakers were the Editor of the New York Times, the Managing Editor of the New York Herald Tribune, Mrs. Roosevelt, the commentator Kaltenborn and numerous other famous journalists. The convention lasted two days. The rest of the week we spent visiting the Museum of Natural History, the Aquarium, lunches at Columbia with college students, an evening at the Waldorf Astoria for dinner, and we lodged at Columbia, guests of a ballet troupe who also entertained us, and an evening of theatre. We had a choice of Radio City Music Hall or a theatre production of the Barretts of Wimpole Street with Katharine Cornell and Brian Ahern. I was the only one choosing the latter, and the teacher chose to go with me so I would not go alone.

On the way home she arranged for a one day stay in Washington, D.C. to visit many of the monuments and a trip to Mount Vernon. All this in 1935 during the great depression. I had sensed throughout the course in Journalism that this teacher was offering college level material and practicum to her fifteen-year-old students. I became more convinced years later when I audited a journalism course at the University of Texas.

George reminded me how much we had been given, and I realized I owed more than ever could be repaid. Not only to her but to him.

The next edition of the paper carried a front-page feature story by George announcing my position as editor. I wish I could remember more, but I remember only the first lead paragraph. It read: Jule Marion Jacobson from her flaming curls to the tip of her toes is an original, and "printer's ink flows through her veins."

I guess the part about the editor must have come second.

In Loving Memory of George Widney

The Writer the Dream Catcher

Did you ever fall in love
with a character you wrote
I mean the one you fashioned
from a sleeping memory?

As you fictionalizd the facts
was it wonderful to see
how you made him change to one
you always wanted him to be?

I started out to write
a true and actual tale
and his true traits seemed sufficient
but my pencil wanted more

For it's ever so exciting
as I made him grow and thrive
and I make him live again
with a memory that's alive.

Chapter 3 – Eugene

The silver engraved invitation read:

Mr. Hammond Gayfer

Requests the pleasure of the company of

Miss Jule Marion Jacobson

On the occasion of a reception at his home

On Dog River....

I forget the rest.

I knew that Mr. Gayfer was the owner of the Department Store bearing his name in downtown Mobile. I learned later that he was well known as a patron of the arts. On this occasion he would be honoring a group of young people active in the Mobile Little Theatre, music, and the arts.

My mother, noting I had nothing suitable to wear for this special event, purchased a yellow accordion pleated silk chiffon tea dress on sale for $5.00 at Hammels Department store. I wore short white gloves and carried a small beaded handbag containing my calling card and a lace trimmed white handkerchief.

A black limousine called for me then picked up another girl whom I didn't know and drove us to the home on Dog River. We were the only passengers.

Sherds – a Mémoire

The long stairway flanked by two stone lions at the base led from the edge of the River to a large room brilliant with light from crystal chandeliers.

Entering the room I was greeted by Mr. Gayfer (apparently there was no Mrs. Gayfer) who introduced us to a small group gathered around the grand piano. The other girl joined this group, and Mr. Gayfer led me to a banquet-size round table laden with little cakes and sandwiches. A crystal punch bowl of fruit juice and champagne surrounded by wine glasses occupied the center of the table. I remember thinking, "Am I old enough to drink champagne?" I was 16. I looked around to see if everyone else was drinking. I nodded to several across the room, the few I recognized from Murphy High School.

A young tall thin blond boy approached me from the other side of the table, glass in hand extended to me and reading a poem from a paper outstretched in the other. I wondered for a moment if this was the intended entertainment.

I took the glass and he continued to recite while waltzing in a circle around me. I asked the name of the poem, and he answered, "I wrote it, it's to you, to you." I was both amused and embarrassed and too inexperienced to know how to respond to his flamboyant behavior. I was not unused to flamboyancy, having let myself go in character several times on the stage, as the time I had to act having a nervous breakdown in a Eugene O'Neill play. But I was unsure how to react to such extravagant display this side of the footlights.

I would have said, "I like to write too." However he continued on, appearing not to require a response from me. So I listened politely, not wishing to upstage or compete with his performance.

Eugene and I were both involved in the Little Theatre productions, I with acting and he with staging the sets, but I never recalled seeing him there.

I remember thinking the bright lights, the table and its appointments, the champagne, and Eugene himself were the same golden color.

At that moment my senior year seemed to be a whirlwind of appearances and performances with no time for really getting to know the others on these occasions.

When I thought about it long afterward, I experienced Mr. Gayfer's reception honoring these spirited young amateurs as a gift more of encouragement than praise, one of the many gratuitous rewards received in those early Mobile years hinting at the future.

For all its opulence the memory of the afternoon at the Gayfer mansion on Dog River was dominated by the startling encounter with this golden boy, the first and last time I met Eugene Walter, Mobile, Alabama's *Renaissance Man*.

The Poet's Phenomenon

The tears that come when reading rhymes
flow from the thoughts you had the times
you poured your feelings into words
from scenes then seen and sounds then heard

And now you feel a strange surprise
when choking throat and brimming eyes
give halt to thoughts that now arise
prompting you to apologize.

The emotional past was done you thought,
that ephemeral moment briefly caught
but somehow lost, forever gone,
your reservoir of words has found.

Chapter 4 – Mary

My belief that opposites in personality can not only get along but also be good for each other originated in my relationship with Mary, whom I met when she came from across the street to welcome me the day my family moved from Atlanta to Mobile. We were the same age, thirteen.

She was more reserved, I was more flamboyant.

She wanted to participate in more activities. I made considered choices and avoided others.

She had more friends than anyone I ever knew. I wanted to be civil to all, but I chose to have fewer close friends.

I think this may have been because she was political on principal. She actually later majored in political science. I found politics exciting but more often distasteful. But when the candidate was a friend I would work for him, and did on several occasions.

She was more candid, allowed herself to be negative, even cynical. I avoided voicing unpleasant realities. I was a Pollyana.

She desired to excel in every pursuit she attempted. I did not feel I had to be the best in every one of my activities. I was often content to just participate.

We both studied piano. She said her reason was "to have an accomplishment." For me it was a pleasant experience for my ear and an emotional experience for my heart.

She acted out her humor, engineering many of the pranks we played for our benefit or on others. I was always hesitant but went along. I expressed humor in writing and joking.

She was always the leader, I was more the follower but also the innovator.

She was an admitted achiever. I was a daydreamer.

She was the senior class President, I was her campaign manager and on the Student Council.

She was president of her dramatics class. I had the lead in the Senior play.

She was more of a conformist. I resisted doing things just because others did so.

She was raised a Baptist. My family was Jewish. She became a Unitarian because of her husband's affiliation. I joined when she invited me to attend the Fellowship and ordered, "Sign the book."

We both were comfortable communicating in words and in writing.

We liked each other. We never hurt each other; we never fought, we never had a falling out. We helped each other and gave to each other. She introduced me to her friends and invited me to join in her activities. We were friends all our lives. We stayed in touch for 71 years. We never forgot each other.

She was the first person to come to my door when we moved to Mobile. I was at her bedside the last hour of her life.

In loving memory

Mary Morgan Duggar Toulmin

l-r: Mary Pillans van Antwerp, Joyce Roche, Jule Jacobson Moon,
Mary Duggar Toulmin, Mary Hall Partridge
and an unidentified graduate

Chapter 5 – My Mother's Fig Tree

My mother loved trees. Growing and tending them was her enterprise. She was sad to leave the peach and plum trees in our yard in Atlanta when the family moved to Mobile in 1932. She was thrilled to find the several Satsuma trees in the new back yard. There were also persimmon and pear trees.

The Poinsettia in the front yard Mother trained to grow into a tree almost as high as our two-story house. Mother taught me that almost any bush could be trained to grow into a tree. Soon we had Japonica trees in the front yard to complement the Azaleas. She was told by the neighbors that azaleas should remain bushes. Mother became quite adept at growing them, but her specialty was trees.

My Mother's favorite was the Fig tree, lush and green and producing large, sweet fruit for her famous preserves for her family and friends.

One day some months after our arrival in Mobile I returned home from school to see my Mother sitting quietly with her hands folded in her lap. The tears in her eyes told me something terrible had happened, and her hands were never just folded without some sewing in them whenever we sat down. When I asked what had happened to make her cry, she said Holcomb our yardman had accidentally cut our hedge bordering our neighbor's yard a few inches lower than usual. The neighbor had become very angry shouting at Mother and blaming her for the incident. Then she went into her house and returned with a chemical solution and poisoned the Fig tree.

Poor, old Holcomb, I thought – he had seemed very old to me – a small, wizened black man, always quiet and diligent. I remember he walked dodderingly along – from years of walking on uneven ground, probably.

We children used to enjoy eating lunch with him and Helen, our maid, on our back porch on Thursdays when he came to work. Helen always made his favorite meal, pork chops and collard greens and corn bread, of course. I suppose that was when I decided this was my favorite meal too.

These happy times were going through my mind as I thought how sad Holcomb must have felt to think he was the cause of "Miss Lily's" distress. Our family was furious because we shared our Mother's grief and hurt feelings and her disbelief that anyone could express anger in such a way on a beautiful living thing. It was our hedge, anyway. I supposed she wanted more privacy from us.

We waited for Mother's reaction to say something, do something. After a long silence she said, "it's a crime to kill a fig tree. For a neighbor to do such a hurtful thing she must be a troubled person who is feeling hurt herself." I guessed Mother believed the neighbor did not need any more hurt from us. Besides, we had been taught retaliation was beneath us.

It was then I learned that people who use their anger to do hurtful and damaging things to innocent creatures are themselves hurting and feel driven to blame others.

Years afterward when I read Harper Lee's "To Kill a Mockingbird," in which she wrote "It's a sin to kill a Mockingbird," I remembered my Mother's words, "It's a crime to kill a fig tree."

Soon after the incident which hurt our family but one which remarkably rallied the whole neighborhood around us – even the other members of the injuring woman's family – Mother planted another fig tree. It was larger and more glorious than the first and furnished fruit for all of our friends in the neighborhood.

The way I saw it my Mother converted her sorrow and disappointment in the planting of that second tree. I was to review this incident many times in my life: "Take the hurt inside, feel it, grieve, face the hurtful actions of another, try to understand them without reciprocating in kind, distill the anger from the hurt of the past and use it to create a positive alternative."

Water Memories

My Mother used to say, "Wind is bad but water is worse." It was years before I was to learn what she meant. I have many memories associated with water, the earliest was as a child in Atlanta being taken by my Father to Piedmont Park to feed the ducks on the pond.

At age 10 I went to Camp Fire Girls Camp in Toccoa Falls, Georgia. At night we paddled canoes on the lake called Silver Lake and sang and danced on its shores by moonlight.

We learned to make headbands Indian fashion, choosing a subject from the environment. My beads were green, brown and blue. I called it earth, mountain and sky. In Cherokee language it would be Katawah and that would be my name.

The next summer we rode the bus to Lake Lure in North Carolina and swam with the fishes. Returning to camp after the trip I chose to make another headband, celebrating these experiences. I chose the sea represented on blue background with white semicircular waves. In Cherokee the name is Yapam.

The next summer we would move to Mobile, which my Father said was near Mobile Bay. We vacationed across the bay in Fairhope. We swam and fished at the Gulf Hunting and Fishing Club on Dog River. That year a big gale swept dolphins into the river, and I remember the thrill of finding myself swimming between two of them, while my Father smiled reassuringly from the pier.

Next year during a hurricane the water came up almost to the level of our house on Bienville Avenue and my young brothers sailed a small boat down our street. Later when I was sailing a waterspout threw me overboard then swirled around the piers tossing them up in the air like matchsticks.

Now it seems the early years in Mobile were overflowing with exciting experiences on the water.

Something to Like About a Storm

Because I believe that something good
Comes out of everything
There must be something good about a storm.
I must admit for me it's about the excitement
I'm the kind of person who enjoys being excited
It's relaxing, refreshing to me.
Some who get excited become anxious –
Not me. I come alive I have to say
I thrive on emergencies, I come into my own
I get to do for people
I don't have so many to do for now.
I get to comfort people
I get to take care of people
I get to use my muscles
With storms come a spur to my creativity
I get to call 911 and take charge
I feel as if I can do almost anything
I get to think I am a small influence in their lives.

What is the Color of a Hurricane?

No, it's not a favorite color – wait
As soon as I say this I realize it is –
The color of Ivan, that's the hurricane I knew
Most fully, the one that took me away to Montgomery
And took my roof when I was away
The color is my favorite for backgrounds,
The color of sand down south and rocks out west
And marshmallow white cornices, always white,
In my old houses

But in Ivan it was bright lightning white
The reflections on the vehicles,
The never ending stream of cars and trucks
On their fearsome trek to Montgomery

I can see them now, the piercing white eyes of headlights
Snailing their way to safety from the storm

Growing Together

When I was two my Mother sang
and started rhythms in my head
when I was three she brought me books
and mystic vistas when we read

She smoothed pink lotion on my hands
the way I knew my Mother then
her hair was gray and very straight
how old she was when I was ten.

Old fashioned shy and slow to speak
not one to venture slow to join
but seeing to it I was not
the way she was so I'd "belong."

She seemed more youthful in my teens
all smart and quick with untold skills
she understood my needs and still
was sympathetic to my whims.

When I was fifty I was stunned
to see how modern she'd become
exhibiting a cleverness
that until now I'd never known.

Her love her humor kept us close
through all our many differences
and now that I am really old
I see how young she really is.

My Father's Time

I missed my chance
I was too young
enthroned in the orb of childhood
afloat in the cocoon of youth
my class
my friend
my play
my dress
but not his time.

I only knew my own.
unable to speak of love
enough
I chanted words of the poets
but had none of my own.

I was not brave enough
to sacrifice my time -
sacrifice his word
his way
his duty as he said -
I was not quick enough to challenge.

And then I was twenty-two and departing
that time there was no time
and now I have the words
oh, I have the words!
and I have the time
but not his time.

Chapter 6 – Lethale

Hers was the most beautiful 17-year-old face I had ever seen, but her dimpled smile seemed only to accentuate the aura of tragedy I saw about her from the moment we met.

I couldn't understand my feelings at the time. Perhaps it was because of her large dark eyes and dark hair I associated with legendary beauties of literature and opera. It could have been her name, Lethale and the nickname her friends used, "Lethal." I couldn't help thinking her mother should have added another "e" to her name. Later she said the same thing about the spelling of mine.

We inherited each other as roommates in the dormitory at midterm when her first term roommate, a friend from her hometown dropped out of the University. We became instant friends, sharing our thoughts and feelings about our involvements, including our parents. Hers were divorced. Mother and daughter were a devoted and affectionate pair, but she was also attached to her father. I thought this must be the basis of Lethale's gift for amiability and compatibility with friends. Lethale had several close friends as I did, but there was a special bond between us. Her intended college course was pre-med. Her leisure time was spent drawing charcoal studies but she seemed as interested in my writing. Although I was committed to majors in geology and anthropology, I managed to take poetry and writing courses, and I had leanings toward the medical area also.

"We're quite alike," she said, "in that we both choose science and the arts. I have to admit," she added, "but we're really different physically. You're tall with a good figure and blond curls, and I'm short with dark, straight hair. And worst of all, flat chested," laughing.

"But we both have the same kind of legs, fat," I countered.

Lethale would join me after class and ask about my writing, the subjects of my composition class, and insist on my reading themes to her.

Once the theme assignment was for a descriptive piece. The professor had emphasized that he intended to challenge our ability to write descriptively.

My response was immediate. I would use Lethale as the subject and make up a story based on a description of her features and characteristics.

I had always done this as a child. It began with long trips in Atlanta on the streetcar to the parks and the roundabout route to downtown. When an individual would board the car I'd get an impression of the person and to pass the time to dream up a story to fit what I saw in the person.

Lethale was an easy subject. I began with the description of a beautiful, dark haired young woman dressed in a lace-trimmed filmy white gown. I entered the room to find her lying on a chaise lounge, her eyes closed and her hands folded. She was surrounded by papers and books and a tablet of charcoal drawings and some crayons. There was a brass cage holding a canary. I left it for the reader to decide whether illness, death, or invalidism was the reason for her stillness.

I remember nothing of the rest except the last paragraph: "Reluctantly after a long while I left the room. The stillness was suddenly broken by the chiming of the hall clock blending with the goodnight song of her canary. I must not forget to feed him."

I told Lethale that the professor must have liked it because he asked me to come back after class and read the story to him. She was delighted and after hearing it asked for a copy, which I gave her.

After graduation we maintained our friendship through occasional letters. We were both on the move. I married in Texas before the outbreak of World War II. Lethale was to be married a month later in Tennessee. Then my husband's geophysics job moved us to Oklahoma. Weddings were brief at the time, with the usual associated extended festivities deleted. Everything else seemed to move with and be obscured by the war. Lethale and I lost touch.

Several years later after graduation I learned from a mutual friend why Lethale had not written. On the eve of her wedding, traveling to the wedding site, her car went over the edge of a mountain road.

She became paralyzed and confined to a wheel chair. She was in rehab for months. Her fiancé begged her to marry him. It was like her to think of his welfare instead of her own. In spite of his continued pleading she refused him. Finally he realized there was no hope for their future together.

I was stunned by the news. What should I do? If I called or came by would she feel as I did – upset by the connection to my story? Somehow I felt responsible. It was absurd, but the memory of the circumstances was too strong.

I then tried to locate her without success, and soon became involved with another move that made it impossible for me to get away.

Sherds – a Mémoire

Years later, it would be ten years now since our college days, my husband was transferred to Houston which was not too far from Port Arthur, her hometown.

I called and her mother answered and responded with an invitation to visit as soon as possible.

I drove to her home and approached the small brick house with strong mixed feelings. I wanted to see her but was fearful at the prospect of encountering a depressing situation. I entered the short entryway and down the hall to her bedroom.

Lethale sat in a wheelchair. She was dressed in a pretty lace trimmed white pinafore looking as beautiful as I remembered her. A yellow canary was in a white cage close to the open window.

Charcoal crayons were tied to her hands and she had just finished one of her portraits. She smiled and greeted me in the same way as when we were girls – swiftly and brightly, her voice bubbling over with joy. The accident had taken its toll on her body but not her attitude or depth of feeling.

She had been spending her time engaged in drawing portraits of the soldiers returning from the war. She was the darling of the local veterans' associations. She was a celebrity and I knew a brave and heroic one.

Finally she turned the conversation to me and my activities. I told her I'd been asked to play the piano at the Houston School for the Deaf to supply a rhythmic background for the children as they marched and danced.

"No," she said, "I mean tell me about your writing." She particularly wanted to discuss the composition written about her. She said she had lost her copy and had hoped for a replacement. "I can't remember much about it after all these years, but I remember I liked it so much and it was your portrait of me."

Today 60 years after that meeting, I cannot remember whether I sent the story or not. I know I did not want to send it. I even may have told her I couldn't find it.

This is how I would have wished to resolve that haunting coincidence. Or was it?

In Loving Memory of Lethale Capland

Intolerance the Eighth Deadly Sin

Mobile was the place
my first meeting with refugees,
teenage girls like me in 1934
Lisa and Gretchen pretty Jewish escapees
from Hitler's Germany where
their physician father
and physician mother
were taken from their fine house
into the yard and shot.

Rescued by their uncle
and brought to his fine house
on Government Street.
I recall particularly their sweet voices
not guttural nor harsh
like those I'd heard in movies
but soft and sweet when speaking
to each other and to me,
how sweetly spoken when extolling
the qualities of the Germany they fled
making no pretense of hiding
their homesickness for their country.

Intolerant, I would feel indignation
revulsion at their references,
defence of their culture
and seeming lack of gratitude
for being alive and sheltered
here in luxury.
how hard it was for me
to understand them and feel close
I learned the meaning of foreigner

They saw the cherished vestiges
of the Confederacy
the ante-bellum manse the old customs

the speaking of the past
as if it still existed
the lingering emotional stances
of the Southerners
they saw as strange and backward.

I saw these remnants as antiquated,
the old ones needing to nourish
their memories to talk over
what they could no longer embrace.

Before a barrier of apparent feeling
of national superiority
so typically Teutonic as I'd been told,
how could I a child of free America
comprehend the reverence
of children driven out by countrymen
their parents killed in the name
of that country.

This child of Georgia and Alabama,
sojourner in Texas, Oklahoma
South Carolina, California and Kentucky -
soul native of them all,
long ago acknowledged our own
and often cruel and sorrowful
as well as glorious history.

Now, finally after more than seventy years
I think how like my own
were my young friends' pride and allegiance
to their native land.

Chapter 7 – Isabel

Isabel was a pretty, petite brunette secretary to the Director of an agency where I was employed for a few years in the late 1940's. She usually wore dark blue or black suits with white collars and cuffs which complimented her dark hair and brown eyes. The only embellishments were her large gold hoop earrings, which I thought must be her sartorial escape hatch.

She was in charge of the files and bookkeeping and all things pertinent to the efficient running of the office. She was methodical and punctual. If any one of the other employees lost, misplaced, or needed any item she was the one to find it, no project was too difficult or challenging. Her boss referred to her as the perfect secretary. She would only blush and smile in response. I never knew a more competent person who obviously did not realize her worth.

I came to know her through our occasional meetings at the employees' coffee table. Our encounters soon became visits as our conversations opened up our mutual interests in music, writing and art. She lived alone and I discovered how important her home environment was to her, the place where she spent most of her time crafting artful additions to her house.

She talked about her remodeling projects and I was not surprised to learn that she was the carpenter, plumber, and electrician.

Soon after this discussion she invited me over to see the work on her latest project, a basement area turned into a recreation room.

The house was small, a modestly appointed bungalow, circa 1930. The entry hall was in colors of burnt orange and blue-green, a brass plant stand and an antique carved gilt mirror framed the oak front door. A narrow, steep stairway led from the kitchen to the basement.

"This is my pièce de resistance," she said proudly, as she pointed out the artful, brightly colored painted design on the floor. I noted it represented measures of music portrayed in an undulating arc about 4 feet long and a foot high. I did not immediately recognize the score.

"It's my favorite," she said as she identified Bizet's Carmen. "The music is the fate theme."

My reaction to her comment was one of shock and a feeling of malaise. I couldn't think to ask – while she continued to describe the work remaining to be finished on the walls – why the fate theme, that haunting sequence of notes that weave throughout the entire Opera, recurringly signaling doom and death.

Why not I kept asking myself the Habanera, the melodic, exciting, teasing taunting love lyric sung by the taunting flirtatious, daring Carmen, or the aria of love and remembrance of home sung by the soldier Jose's childhood sweetheart, as she pleads for Jose to leave for home with her, or even the triumphant Toreador song praising the Toreador and heralding the glorious end to the bull fight, or even any of the other happy songs of adventure sung from time to time by the company chorus?

All I could think of was how it would be for me to encounter this dolorous theme every day. However, Isabel's tone as she spoke sounded as if she thought of the theme as a happy melody. It must have been that her tone reflected her feeling of accomplishment. It certainly was a work of art. She continued to describe the rest of the proposed construction including the electrical outlets.

It was late and I wanted to leave. "Let me serve you coffee in the kitchen. It's all finished there," she said. It was certainly not a typical kitchen of the 1940's. There was a timeless air, with plain décor except for the burnt orange and blue-green color scheme and black wrought iron table and two chairs. Not like my own kitchen in red and white and counter accoutrements of the time, homespun pot holders and wooden wall ornaments fashioned from cooking utensils!

"Good luck with your work, I'll see you tomorrow," I said leaving.

However, I was feeling overwhelmed with something I could only identify as dread, as I thought about the symbolism of the painting. A premonition – no it was my habit of dramatizing my perceptions of situations, infusing symbolic meanings.

Isabel did not show up at work the next day. She was never late so I wondered what could be keeping her. Before I could ask the director he said she had been found dead, electrocuted by a defective drill as she worked in her basement room where somehow a leaking pipe flooded the floor.

"A terrible accident," he said, "how could such a competent, efficient person have made such a mistake?"

I could not answer. All I could think about and still remember with sadness today is the musical score emblazoned on the floor.

Why Do I Write?

I like to tell a story
I long to reach some kindred soul with it
perhaps like one of theirs
so they will know me
and something of what
my generation, fast retreating was.

It is a peaceful struggle
this enterprise, a quiet vocation
summoning up thoughts
familiar yet somehow new,
each one a meditative mission
opening up unexpected awareness.

I like to explore the often messy,
always nebulous mental field
hoping to extract a crystalline find.

But most of all I like to putter
to dabble to wander
in the wondrous galaxy of words.

Chapter 8 – Kiowa Legacy

It was in the early spring of 1942 in Norman, Oklahoma. My husband James was putting his recently earned Master's degree in geology to work as a geophysicist with the Carter Oil Company. I had received my Master's too in geology from the University of Texas, but now was eager to enter into the career of domesticity, specifically cooking and sewing.

We had been residents of Norman for several months, during which time we had taken all our meals at the local café. James insisted that I should not try to cook, as I had no experience. I contended that I had a cookbook and my Mother's continual commentary on her cooking in my head and these qualified me to be ready for the apprenticeship. I cannot take credit for winning the argument, however, because the day before at Sunday dinner in the café James found a cockroach in his salad.

At 22 years old I would be shopping alone for the first time. While James was exploring the subsurface for oil, this was my exploration – the grocery store.

I set out on foot to walk the 8 blocks from our apartment. Our first three-room home was nothing special, but apartments were scarce in this small town. I forget the size, but compared to Mobile, my hometown, it was a village.

Walking and looking at Mobile's Victorian and ante-bellum houses was a favorite pastime, but here the houses were small and devoid of beautiful architectural elements and design that I had always taken for granted. These were mostly bungalows, which I thought literally meant small houses, plain with no brick or stucco facades, only wood and dull white or a monotonous beige color, or was it only the brownish red dust that seemed to overlay everything? No lofty Junipers or Cedars either for shrubbery out front, only small plants set here and there in no particular pattern and appearing dry and scrubby. And indeed this was due to the dust storms of recent years.

Approaching downtown I noticed the buildings all very much alike at the top, lacking creative individuality, except for the painted store signs. They reminded me of the old towns depicted in the wild west movies – all plain board and rectangular facades.

The window of the general store displayed garments, shoes, and even folded underwear in no particular pattern, as if they were accidentally dropped rather than placed.

Two manikins wearing dresses were bald, eyes in their wooden heads staring straight ahead, a bulky tube-like body attached with no arms and two planks criss-crossed on the floor serving for feet. Old-timey I thought, like the ones I remembered from my Uncle Henry's department store in Camden, South Carolina where I visited many summers as a child. A far distant relation it seemed to me from the marcelled wigged stylish manikins wearing New York fashions in the windows at Hammel's in Mobile. I didn't know much about grocery stores, but dress shops - that was a different story.

The hardware store, on the other hand, looked familiar, a coffee brown board and batten exterior with farm implements and burlap feed sacks stacked outside.

In the next block at last was the grocery store, another square building painted red and white with a large front window through which one could see large baskets of fruit and a smaller sign, SAFEWAY above. The doors were situated at the corner of the store, providing two-way access and were open.

I felt bewildered as I entered this town's largest grocery store, largely because my day's allowance for food was one dollar, along with the cautionary advice to be careful spending it. Moreover I had no idea how much this would cover. As it turns out this was to be my allowance for ten years, and I became adept at managing.

The store was small, as were the bins containing the produce, the shelves narrow with neat array of cans and bottles, the wooden floor was bare of varnish but clean. The glass light fixtures were old fashioned, twentyish, round with embossed flowers similar to the ones we had at home in our bedrooms and kitchen in Mobile.

I walked down the first aisle looking at the produce and felt pleased with myself that I recognized most of the vegetables. Potatoes first, I thought. I picked one up in each hand. One was larger. Which one for supper I wondered? I must have spent some time shifting my attention from one to the other, when I was interrupted by a tall handsome gentleman in the black suit approaching, tipping his black Stetson hat (I knew it was a Stetson, because I had lived in Texas for 6 years and Texas was big Stetson country). Two black braids hung to his shoulders. This did not surprise me, as I knew Oklahoma was Indian country. I had minored in anthropology and was friends with several Indians in my classes.

"May I be of assistance?" he asked.

I faltered, "I'm sort of new at this." Might as well be honest. Whereupon he began to tell me about the store, the quality of its produce and its brands. I had accompanied my Mother to the Piggly Wiggly and A&P in Mobile when I was a child, but I paid little attention to the purchasing. I usually looked for and greeted friends who might be in the store.

I listened fascinated as he continued. I knew this was really important.

"Now these potatoes are the freshest, and reasonable too. You can rely on the house brands, no need to spend more on these," pointing to the two brands of catsup on the shelf.

Aisle by aisle we went as he elaborated on the store's offerings. I finally ventured a choice. I made my decisions based on his suggestions as to brand and price and ended with a beginning pantry: a small sack of flour with a lady in a flowered hat stamped on the cloth, two potatoes, two onions, a pound of coffee, baking powder, and lard (for biscuits I hoped), a pound of hamburger, salt and garlic. And 10 cents left over. Milk was delivered and put in the icebox by the milkman, and paid to him by the week.

My host waited while I finished at the cash register. He must have come in for cigarettes, because I don't remember him carrying any groceries.

He led me outside to his car, a black Cadillac limousine.

"I'd like you to meet my wife," he said. She and several children were sitting in the back seat. She wore braids, longer than her husband's and a colorful blanket drawn around her shoulder. I'm sure I stared at it, because it was similar to the one my Mother gave me when I left for the University in 1936. I'm not sure where she acquired it, but I remember she was proud of her Indian blanket, and I still had it. The one I was staring at this day was more gaily colored than mine.

"Mrs. Moon is new to Norman," her husband told her.

"Welcome, welcome," she said, smiling.

Unlike her husband she spoke with an accent.

We talked briefly about Norman as a good place to live, then said our goodbyes.

"I hope we meet again. I will be happy to be of assistance in any way in the future," he said.

He was as good as his word.

The experiences and people of those early Oklahoma years were among the most delightful and important of my life, but the tall handsome stranger who assumed the role of host in his locale and who taught me the elements of grocery shopping is the one I remember most fondly.

Chapter 9 – The Role of Paleontology

When my husband began his two years of study toward the PhD in geology at the University of Texas, I enrolled in the Department of English for several courses, which when added to my graduate and undergraduate courses in the English Department would bring me almost up to candidate level for a PhD in English. I completed these in one semester and now needed only German, a course in old English and the dissertation, which I planned on finishing in two years.

My idea for this dissertation was the combining of folklore with anthropology and archeology, which had been my minors to the major in geology. The anthropology department head, Dr. Gilbert Mc Allister, approved. Dr. J. Frank Dobie, the noted Texas folklore author, would be the supervisor in charge and I was sure he would give his approval. Unfortunately he was in England on sabbatical, so it was necessary for me to apply to the Dean of Arts and Sciences, my Shakespeare professor. He disapproved of my subject and suggested a more classical, traditional one – "Hollingshead's sources of Shakespeare."

It was one of those crossroads. For me it was anthropology, archeology and folklore or nothing. My husband heard that an Instructorship in paleontology was available and suggested my name to the head of the Department of Geology, who had been my professor for two courses when I was a student. I was immediately offered the position from 1947 – 1949 which required teaching laboratory sections in invertebrate paleontology, a required sophomore course. Several of the instructors had not at this time returned from their military assignments, hence the opportune opening for me, a 27 year old female with no prior University teaching experience except as an assistant in the departments of geology and anthropology and part-time tutoring geology students when I was a graduate student. I was assigned to four laboratory sections.

I was not prepared for the position, although I had taken four requisite paleontology courses. I certainly was not prepared for the brilliant students enrolled in my sections who were already competent on the subject, being amateur fossil collectors. And then there were the sons of geologists who began asking advanced questions on the subject! However, they were surprised when I encouraged their participation.

The students happened to be all male, ranging in age from 20 to 37. Nearly all were enrolled supported by the G.I. bill, the legislative educational grant provided for World War II veterans. There were former privates, corporals, sergeants and one captain. One of these would become Chairman of the Paleontology Department, another would become President of U. S. Shell Oil Company.

Here was a unique group, even an historically unique group. I viewed this group sometimes as students, sometimes as colleagues, sometimes as children and always as audience. Group and audience I understood from my childhood and young adulthood experiences in the amateur theatre. In a large group of people assembled for a learning experience there is always the performer, the performance, and the audience.

My Father, the general sales manager of the International Paper Mill during the 1930s and 1940s, was also involved in the training of newly hired young employees in the sales department. From him I learned the connection between teaching and salesmanship. I would need both. From the very first day the students demonstrated their negative feelings about the school experience and being in my classes. Frequent angry outbursts occurred, stemming from pent-up emotions from their wartime experiences at Anzio, Guadalcanal, the Bataan march and others.

One day a former master sergeant angrily pulled off his shirt to show me the scars on his back from lashings. It was his way to counter my authority over some issue which I now have forgotten. He apparently saw me as an unwelcome authority figure. I had no such intention. I tried in my response to let him see my empathy toward him. His look softened and he slowly sat down. I wanted the students to know I was not trying to win a battle, only their interest. Many showed their contempt or resistance in raging responses or in very audible snickering. Generally they did not see the necessity for studying fossils, which they viewed as irrelevant to the business of exploration for oil which was their final goal. Although their immediate task was to achieve as a student one of the basic subjects of paleontology they, having been out of the mainstream for years, were anxious to get on with the end goal.

I had my task too, so I stood my ground citing rules and regulations set out by the University and teaching the scientific methods for identification and applications of the specimens put out each day on their lab tables. I recognized my limitations and did not attempt to cover up my missteps and errors but acknowledged them. Interestingly enough when this happened the students responded with respectful attention. Each day was exciting if a struggle.

A breakthrough in teacher-student relations came, initiated by a six foot four redheaded former master sergeant. This occurred when a professor in charge of other lab sections entered the room when I was going through my usual 15-minute introductory lecture prior to the work for the day. I was talking and illustrating my subject on the blackboard behind the lecture desk. The professor darted in front of me, picking up first one and then another of the fossils I had arranged on the desk to discuss and was examining them under his hand lens. The student stood up suddenly, banged his book on the table and exclaimed, "I'll be damned," and strode out of the room, slaming the door as he left. No one said a word and the professor turned abruptly and left the room.

I realized instinctively the value of such behavior in group process. The sergeant had thrown down the gauntlet. The class from this time on rallied and was supportive of me when there was a verbal attack by any staff or classmate. And the word must have gone out to other lab sections. The friendly atmosphere was palpable.

I worked hard to make the course which required much memory work interesting. I used experiential and role-playing methods in my teaching. My goal was to enable the student to insert himself in the imaginary process of discovering the fossils and feeling the conditions under which he found them.

I wrote such test questions as the following: "The sun is sinking over the hills of a small central Texas village. You are walking on ground of chalky white limestone in which there are many specimens of a genus of Pelecypoda. To what era and period would you assign the formation, and what is its name?" The students would laugh at such questions, but they would learn.

I also gave lectures once a week in the auditorium to all of my laboratory sections. The hour was mid-afternoon, and I remembered when I was a student that I had difficulty staying awake during the times the light went dim and the professor would show slides and discuss the characteristics of every fossil. I had to admit it was a tedious performance. I tried to make the lectures as interesting as possible, but I used a few psychological and visual aides to interrupt the long detailed presentations. For example I would suddenly play the record of a marching band to accompany the scene of a progression of fossils in a formation. They would sit up and become alert to watch for what else might pop up.

Sometimes I would flash a picture of a movie star in a bathing suit before a fossil with several curves in the shell would be shown. There was much in my dramatic armormentarium to insure their attention.

I told them there would be no tricks or surprises on the weekly pop quizzes. I said however that I expected them to learn the geologic time-table and know it "like the back of your hand." I promised to ask it on the first pop quiz. The timetable is a vertical list of eras and periods representing the age of the rocks in the earth's crust starting at the bottom of the list with the earliest rocks, the Pre-Cambrian (Archeozoic and Proterozoic) to the latest and youngest (the Present and Recent). Each quiz would have this question. Many would miss it. "I told you I would ask it," I said. Their answer, "We didn't believe you." The question emerged on the next quiz. Many missed it again. I continued as promised until finally everyone made a hundred on the quiz. Then one of the students asked, "Why do you do this, giving us the answer ahead of time?"

"I want you to learn it. It's essential."

When I graded their papers I noticed the students kept losing points for misspelling the terminology. The professor in charge of all the classes took two points off for each misspelled word on the general exams. The students complained, "That's not fair, and besides the words don't make sense." Their response handed me my next assignment. I would teach them Greek and Latin. Scientific nomenclature is universal and therefore in classical language which is universal. The translation would indicate the description of the fossil, which of course made identification possible. Example: the genus Exogyra, a fossil characteristic of the Cretaceous period, ex= out and gyra= turn. The fossil's body is turned outward, and so it appears. I would also point out similar well-known words, for example, exit.

At the end of the semester the professor, a former Navy Captain, came into my classroom with his grade book to complain about my performance, "Your grades are too high, higher than all the other lab sections. You must be too easy on them. What exactly are you doing?" I answered, "Teaching a little Greek and Latin to increase their understanding." He shook his head, laughing as he left.

I later admitted I added two points to every student's grade at the end of the semester. Papers were graded in sessions by me as well as by a number of student assistants. Errors were made frequently, particularly when the questions were of the discussion type and required the assistants to make judgments about the quality and quantity of answers. I wanted to be sure the errors and omissions would not penalize the students. The professor did not approve of this unorthodox addition to the grading system and accused me of being "too generous." From my point of view I figured I owed these World War II veterans every consideration and benefit of the doubt. The grades were not changed.

I cannot detail all the dramatic experiences of those two years, teaching those veterans of World War II who transformed themselves into college students. Every day brought challenges and opportunities for creative applications to lesson assignments. It was a sobering task for me to dare to attempt to teach them, since some of them were more experienced in fieldwork than I. But more than that they were war veterans. In the beginning I focused on the usual teacher-student relationship. But soon, as their responses to me revealed their delayed reactions to combat experiences I had to learn how to respond to these emotional situations. They were heroes, and I couldn't forget it, and their desire to succeed inspired me to inspire them.

The most unexpected reward was my beginning to realize the need for support from mental health professionals for the returning military personnel from the wars and their adjustment to civilian life. I owe to them the start of my interest and involvement in the field of mental health and mental illness. From them I learned some of the elements of how to approach and work with disturbed people. I included these as I became a family therapist to both individual families and groups of families who have needs for coping with the exigencies and tragedies of living.

Four years later I would become a Red Cross volunteer in the Wichita Falls State Hospital and a volunteer in the effort to establish a community mental health center. All these experiences led to my return to the University of Texas as a student of social work with emphasis on psychiatric studies and applications for family therapy.

A Boulder Thrown from a High Bridge

Standing high on a bridge
overlooking the scene below
of the racing caravan
including me in my brand new
very small car, three or four of them
with arms raised –
in greeting I thought –
when suddenly one hurled
a brick-size boulder
at me which made a loud crack
at eye level on
my windshield which did not break.

Thoughts raced along with me
as I looked for a safe place to stop.
was this some sport
some aim at skill
akin to skimming smooth rocks
on lake water
some planned exploit of energy
born of the young not able yet
to own the mechanical icon
of our culture?

Or unable to procure a gun
those fingers itching for a weapon
or some caricature emulation
of Goliath now bested
by another David?

Was this some joke
a funny thing to watch –
an old woman
in a hapless moment
or even pain and injury?

Minutes later far enough away
for me to breathe
and stop to examine
what surely must be some damage
I saw with amazement no mark at all
from that cruel adolescent revelry,
so on I went wondering
why did those strangers
want to hurt my little car?

Chapter 10 – James

The subject matter of this chapter does not lend itself to poetry or vignettes which to me are the most fun to write. Since I favor leaning toward the bright side I like happy endings. A clinic supervisor once said to me, "You are too positive, you need to look and see the client's weaknesses." She was right of course. Still, sometimes my spontaneous positive attitude has the advantage of keeping one's spirits up. For example returning home from the hospital next day after a mastectomy, I felt good, even elated because my condition did not require chemotherapy or radiation. Seeing this result as a great gain, I never shed a tear for my loss.

Favoring the positives and habitually avoiding the negatives was a handicap in my relationship with my husband.

This is a story about one of the two talented and tormented men whom I built my life around. I was married to the first for seventeen years. I lived with the second for almost twenty. What I write here about their childhoods I know only from what they told me, little by little over the years. They had family backgrounds somewhat in common, but in the matter of their personalities they couldn't have been more dissimilar.

They were both raised during the Depression of the 1930's, in farm families which were poor before, during, and after the depression years. They both had lost their fathers in early childhood years and experienced life with neurotic, diffident, and often, if unintentionally, harsh and punitive mothers. Fortunately they had caring and loving older sisters who were able to help them from time to time and communicated love, but with little expressions of affection.

As for me, I was raised by parents who tended to be overprotective but whose aim was putting the happiness and welfare of their children above their own. It was clear to us that they wanted to provide for us more than they were given in their own childhoods. I assumed all educated and church-going families could do no other.

I was married for the first time at age 22 to James, two years older. We met when we were both geology majors at the University of Texas at Austin, Texas. Although we dated occasionally for two years, I knew little about him, which was not unusual in those days, unlike young people who had grown up in the same town and attended school together, or like young people today who often live together before marriage. This handsome young man possessed no material assets, no house, no car, no money. He had spent his last $5.00 on an orchid for me for the wedding, at the insistence of his older sister. The part about the "insistence" should have been a red flag, but I only knew that I observed his brilliance, he was hard-working, and ambitious with a Master's degree in geology. I had no doubt that he would be successful in his profession. From little to go on I assumed that he intended to be a good husband. When I told him I wanted four children he agreed.

We had interest in archeology as well. But the condition that often undermines compatibility was that we were opposites in personality, temperament, cultural backgrounds and personal tastes.

I was used to being able to discuss needs and problems and confiding in those I was close to. Generally James looked at things being right or wrong and "no discussion." Since good communication is essential to making compromises I learned later we were doomed.

He was referred to by our friends as "quiet." I soon discovered he was introverted – a term I think aptly descriptive, and task-oriented – a trait I came to abhor. I consider myself extroverted, needing family and friends involved in my life. Hobbies and interests in both the arts and sciences for me were enjoyed as a respite from work and for my feeling of well being. James said he had enough fun out in the field, working as a geologist. I enjoyed exploring as a geologist too, at the time, only not as a sole activity.

Nevertheless I convinced myself in the beginning that we complemented each other and would learn to adapt to each other. In spite of my knowing some terminology from my psychology courses, my little knowledge was indeed a dangerous thing. I had been aware of the need for accommodation in marriage. I thought my parents were a good example. They learned to share interests in common, were different in many ways and had some separate interests, which the other appreciated and approved of.

From my family I knew that diversity can lead to an interesting life. I thought then, which is a well known view now, that spouses can benefit from each other having interests in common as well as different or separate interests. I found out James did not agree.

I think now learning to share must somehow be connected to allowing differentness in another. James was eight years younger than his next older sibling, the other three sisters were much older. And he was the only boy. I imagine he didn't have to do much sharing.

The mental model I had of men derived from observing, listening to, and enjoying times with my Father. He was dedicated to his position as a paper company salesman. You could feel his pride as he talked about the challenges with "tough customers" and "winning them over" to his trade. I always believed that his tolerance of differentness and his great sense of humor were two of the qualities responsible for his success in his business. He also thought it was important to be liked.

My brothers and I were certainly different and had different kinds of interests. Mother preached tolerance, especially to me – the oldest and only girl. Peace-making not arguing was taught and fighting was forbidden.

My parents were music lovers – my paternal grandfather was a violinist. Music of several kinds was a big part of our family life. We had a radio, a piano, and a Victrola with records ranging from ragtime to opera. They applauded but did not insist or push us into piano, voice or ballet, band, and even elocution, a popular trend activity for girls in those days. My brothers were athletic – as I was not. They liked golf and we all played tennis.

My father loved the water and most everything Florida. The paper company made the large company boats available to the employees for deep sea fishing. The only thing I ever caught was an alligator gar. Nearly every drive to somewhere in Georgia and later Alabama became a fantastic experience for us. Our Father made sure we experienced special adventures to remember, like the air shows at Lakewood Park in Atlanta where the high and low-flying barnstormers performed on the weekends. We learned first hand the horror of a stunt gone wrong when we witnessed the female parachutist who let go of two parachutes and then fell into the trees when the third failed to open. Then there was the day we stood in line among the adoring throng waiting to get a glimpse of Charles Lindberg on his triumphant tour through the country after his 1927 solo flight from New York to Paris. All we could have was a glance, a flash of cropped golden hair and sunburned face as the convertible sped through the crowded Atlanta street. I wonder now if my Brother Lee, who became a Naval fighter pilot in 1942, and Brother Frank, who became a paratrooper in the Army Air Corps, also in the war, would date their interest in aviation back to those days. Lee was 6 at the time and Frank 4. From that time on they were absorbed with aviation.

Sherds – a Mémoire

There were vacation trips every summer, the first to Pensacola Beach as soon as we were settled in Mobile.

Then there was the "big Florida trip," in 1934, which took us from Mobile to Tampa south and down to Miami and up the east side – the "Tamiami Trail". Our father promised us a spectacular sight at one of the large hotels. We became very quiet as we drove up to the fancy buff and coral colored Spanish style building with the large lobby door opened to the outside veranda. Inside there were real palm trees lining the walls and birds, canaries I think, singing in dozens of cages.

There was a sobering lesson to be learned about the Depression from this trip. After driving along a stretch of empty roadway that I remember as a desert, we passed many large hotels, chalk white and all characterized by the same stark front grounds scene overgrown with tall weeds. Bright shiny new bathtubs, toilets, sinks and ranges which had been shipped and were then dropped in front of the doors of the empty hotels looked like so many scattered, abandoned tombstones. That scene has stayed with me and resurfaced frequently during the current housing crisis.

Birthdays were always special occasions too, marked by our Mother allowing us to choose our favorite cake on our day. We celebrated all the holidays with a feast especially Thanksgiving, because it occurred in the same week as our Father's birthday. We celebrated Hanukkah and Christmas. I don't remember anyone complaining about commercialism then. I suppose people were happy about anything the merchants could do to enliven the desperate times. We were still experiencing the Depression as long as I lived in Mobile. I was aware we did not suffer, as we read about the soup and bread lines up north. What I remember most about gifts was choosing those for our favorite teachers.

Christmas time was uncomfortable for James. He said it was a waste of time and money. I thought he was uncomfortable with the sentiments of the holiday. He would attend his family's dinner on that day out of a sense of duty. I bought small gifts for his family out of the $25.00 my parents sent me. I listened to the family members' wishes during the year and made note of them. One year my Mother-in-law kept requesting a map of the City, which she addressed to her daughters. At the Christmas gathering I presented her with a map wrapped up in paper and ribbon. The map cost only 50 cents, but I was proud that I could give her something she wanted. James was angry and embarrassed by the "cheap" gift. His mother was thrilled, she said, to at last get her wish. I only wished he could be happy.

Sherds – a Mémoire

The philosophy in our family was that being poor in America was no hindrance to obtaining success either in marriage or one's occupation if you worked hard at it and put a high priority on love. James worked his way through college waiting on tables in dormitories, and I admired him for it. He had little of what I considered the basics for a happy childhood and none of the extras. So when I married him I didn't realize how many of my beliefs about married life I projected on my husband.

After a few months of marriage he began to lose interest in his new job. It certainly wasn't because he was unsuccessful in his work. Quite the contrary, his crew Chief complimented him frequently on his field exploration. I observed he seemed to feel uncomfortable working with the other crew members. He would comment that one or two were "ok."

In spite of having discovered an oil field, he was unable to adapt to situations which depended on getting along with his superiors with whom he felt uncomfortable at work. When he was offered a vice-presidency with the geophysical company he had been with only a year, he turned it down. When I asked him what he objected to he said, "I don't like all that responsibility." When I attempted to understand his thinking further he said, "I just turned it down. I just don't want it, and that's all there is to it."

Our social life in the first five years was made possible by the geophysical crew families who were old hands at "doodle-bugging" – geophysical life – and liked a good time. We lived closely together and moved as a unit from town to town. There were picnics and parties and sometimes cards and dominoes and always beer. When the men were working a long distance from home, sometimes overnight, the women would carpool to another little village nearby to explore the stores. I regularly presented myself to the local Red Cross unit to roll bandages, knit afghans for the sailors or whatever was needed for a volunteer to do.

I enjoyed crew life. I was often able to include past favorite activities. Once I was asked to write a newsletter which would be sent to the other company crews so that others would be in touch with the happenings of our crew. On one crew I drifted into a job helping some of the families find places to live. The ones with children were often rejected by the landlords who were hesitant to rent their wartime makeshift apartments to "oil people" in the first place. They were "too likely to up and leave without notice." More often than not their places were too small for a family of five or six. I would introduce myself as recently graduated from the University, obtain a place for us and then persuade them to rent to the families.

Sherds – a Mémoire

When I became accustomed to the sudden disruptive moves to unknown locations, I began to view them with excitement and looked forward to exploring the small towns with their quaint old hardware and dry goods stores which still sold what are now regarded as "rare treasure finds."

Occasionally James and I would visit in Texas with his family, who were always kind and accepting of me. We made a few trips to Mobile to visit my family. One day James said, "I really admire your Dad." This rare sentiment revived my hope that at last we would draw closer together, but then the changes to a number of different jobs involved us in moving and settling frequently, in Canada, New Mexico and all involving months of separation.

Following these moves James decided on leaving geophysical exploration and accepted a position as Associate Professor at the University of Oklahoma. This was a good opportunity and I enjoyed the female associations and our pretty little house there. After 6 months he told me he was disappointed in the job, he "didn't like teaching, I've made up my mind to resign." This was the first time he had discussed his feelings about the problems with the work. I took this as an opening for me to express my strong opinions about the matter. I told him I did not think that leaving after such a short time, especially not finishing out the year, would look good on his record. He agreed. Luckily he was able to take on a summer project which was acceptable to the University – a field operation in Alaska. He would have to then teach another 6 months and return the next summer to Alaska. It was on this project that the Prudhoe Bay oil field was discovered. He was instrumental in the explorations of several oil fields in Oklahoma and Texas. This was clearly his forte, but he would only say "I want to be on my own where I can be my own boss."

James was able to maintain this kind of situation until 1949 when he decided to join the Research team in Houston with the Humble Company. Some of my college chums lived there and we would join in volunteer and other activities. Occasionally I would suggest some activity or even a hobby to offer relief from what he said was a boring routine. His reply was, "not my kind of thing." There was a popular song over the airways I recall that I believed was James's theme song, "Johnny One Note."

The baffling thing was that he was capable of doing other things and doing them well. In the small house in Spring Branch, just outside of Houston, I asked if he could make some simple bookshelves. He didn't hesitate, bought the lumber and tools he needed and began to work on them that day. I suggested that instead of constructing a solid board at the end of the shelf that he make several strips into a trellis on the top of which we could place a trailing green plant. He set about building and finished two book shelves in one day. I was thrilled and told him how beautiful they were. He showed no emotion and looked as if he felt no pleasure in the accomplishment. Sometime after that I said I hoped he would suggest making something else for the home, which had no built-ins of any kind. He "thought the house was all right as it was – we don't need to make any improvements." One of the most baffling things about James was this strange kind of unpredictability.

I never knew where I stood with him. He did seem pleased with one thing I did. It amazed me that any time I went to the piano to play he would say "I like to hear you play."

After a year in Houston, James became unhappy with this position in the research department. This time I was not surprised. But I had my own stresses. I was driving home from my job at Schlumberger Well Surveying Corporation as technical librarian when I realized I was having a miscarriage. It was raining hard and getting dark, so I drove quickly on to the lawn and up close to the front porch, ran inside and lay down on the kitchen floor until James came home a short time later. He was furious because I had driven on the lawn and made ruts in the grass. I went to bed for a while and then got up and made supper. We ate in silence. I was more fearful of his anger than any possible problems from my condition. The next day I said, "James, it's time to say good bye."

I divorced James after nine years when the silences and separateness turned into angry threats and pushing me to leave him. I was afraid of his anger and my submissive behavior played into his domineering aggressiveness. I was no longer willing to live in fear. I had tried to get along long enough.

I continued in a job with an Oil Company in Houston for almost two years. During the last year James began writing to me and called often to say how much he liked Wichita Falls where he had moved two years before, after resigning in Houston. He called one day to tell me he had bought a new house in a pretty neighborhood setting where there were other geologists from his company. He wrote that he was entering into all sorts of social activities with the company personnel and their wives. He was even going dancing which he had never enjoyed before. "I'm a different person and I want a different kind of life. I know you will like it here."

I was sure we could make it now. Once again I looked for what I wanted to see. It was 1952. To his credit he made an effort to be happy and sociable. But he was in a new position in a kind of work differing from anything previous with little opportunity for extensive field work.

New kinds of responsibilities and the pressures of living with me became too much and he returned to his old solitary and sullen ways after 6 months.

My brother Frank sent us a beautiful mahogany eight weeks old Dachshund puppy, and he loved that dog. Then we had a female and raised six puppies. He insisted on keeping two and he doted on the three, unfortunately he was rough on them and would hit them when they wouldn't mind. When he returned from the office in the afternoon after work he couldn't wait to play with the dogs. He would open the door and they would rush to it, when he entered they stopped short, looked at him and ran away in three directions. It was a telling sight. I hoped that he would get the message that you can't hurt a dog in anger and expect love in return. He didn't.

I finally got the message and felt our life together was over, but I'd made a promise; and I determined I would not forsake it a second time. I decided to seek satisfaction and approval in my usual ways during and after the war years as a volunteer in the hospitals. When I applied to the Red Cross chapter I was told we were needed at the Wichita Falls State Hospital. The asylum sign and been removed just months before and there was an atmosphere of new and more humane methods of treatment and rehabilitation prevailing.

The marital crisis came early one evening about six o'clock. I called to James in the backyard and told him I was leaving to go to the City National Bank where the other volunteers were counting the money from the city wide mental health drive. He said "You can't go. It's time for supper." I told him, "The supper is in the oven when you are ready. I have to go, I'm the chairperson of the drive." I usually worked on the drive at home, but this time it was necessary for me to leave. "I'll be home at 10 o'clock." James's answer was to tell me, "You can't go."

It was summer; I put on a cotton dress, put $2.00 in a small purse and left in my car.

At 10 o'clock we were finishing counting the money. The drive was a big success. Everyone was congratulating each other. "We made more money than the Cancer Society!" one shouted. The phone rang - it was for me. It was James. I said, "We are through counting and I'm just leaving."

His answer, "Never mind, when you come home the door will be locked." I stood at the phone I guess for some minutes, when the Public Health Nurse noticed my distress. When I told her I couldn't go home, she said, "You come home with me." I left the car parked on the lot.

I heard the next day the word of my situation went out to the members, who were apparently not surprised at the outcome of the evening before. That day I was offered the position of Executive Director of the Mental Health Association. One of the board's psychiatrists offered me the use of one of his cars. I did not go home again.

My second divorce from James marked the beginning of the adventure that took me into the professional mental health field which would continue until my retirement in 1992. I was 39 years old. I would be 58 before I entered into the kind of relationship I had hoped for all my life.

James married again shortly after our divorce. I heard the marriage lasted a year and a half. He married a fourth time, and this one lasted six months.

In Retrospect – a Toast

Here's to the promise
Of that sweet first hello

Here's to the lonely times
Whispering what could be

Here's to the hardships
Making me a woman

Here's to the pain
A boon to my resolve

Here's to the last farewell
Coming none too soon

The Beginning

It happened on Friday night
1960 I believe it was
but definitely Friday
at 11 o'clock precisely
I returned home from working
all day into the night
at my new job –
not much of one – some would say
it paying me only $250 a month-
a satisfying job nevertheless
if one without much future.

Although tired, bone and world weary
I was hungry and wanted supper
not a ham sandwich
not cheese and crackers
not a can of vegetable soup
not even chocolate ice cream
all available at hand
in an instant.

My hunger called for nothing less
than roast beef – pot roast actually –
my own recipe luscious
with mushrooms and onions
seasoned with garlic, horseradish
and red wine.

And there in the refrigerator,
as if by some culinary divinity, beckoning
a small choice cut of beef
but uncooked – the prospect for eating
2 ½ hours away.

And then it came to me!
it was Friday and no schedule
for tomorrow
and no one to say
"It's 11 o'clock!"
no one to say "No that's crazy!"
no one to nag on the morrow
and call me stupid
no one to say "no!" ever again.

And that was the time
the moment irrevocable
that I was freed from my commitment
my illusion
my dream of a conventional lifestyle.
It was 11 o'clock and I
could have pot roast if I wanted to.

And so I set the oven at 350°
and anointed my prize
with the necessary accoutrements
and luxuriating in my newfound independence
which accompanied me
I waited patiently
the 2 ½ hours
for my reward.

Remnants

This house is substitute for home-
the one I built to last my life—
old chandeliers and hardware gleaned
new boards and bricks and tiles handpicked
the shrubbery trees and flowers a gift
from former owners of their toil

materials here are lesser stuff
as particle board to cherry wood
gone are the friends who claimed these chairs
and pets who guarded, played, and reigned,
work with sick folks needing space
with friendly walls and quiet floors.

From only bits and pieces saved
I'll make this house a home – again.

Conflict Surprise

I strive to live each moment
but the future stares me down
my foot's entrenched in my history
I refuse to bring it round.

I exult in every hour
no less because I'm caught
fore and aft in bondage
from what my fates have wrought.

Just when my mood's submerging
from what may be in store
a sly reward's forthcoming
from some forgotten lore.

Museum

Come see the art show in my house
on every surface I display
my avocations, loves, and works –
and follies when I lost my way.

If you would know me do not glance
but gaze and linger when you look
my house is metaphor for me
my life's an open picture book.

Chapter 11 – Life Change: Prologue Confederate Home, the Hospital

It was early in 1963, in the days before every talk show host became everyman's therapist and every comedy show illustrated the value group process has on people with problems. It was the time before it became the fashion to urge the senior members of our society to keep their minds agile and their bodies young. It was a time when geriatric patients were considered unable to make use of advanced psychiatric treatment; little old ladies in tennis shoes were not credited with a fashion movement but considered a joke; and men were urged if not pushed to retire in their fifties and pointed toward the rocking chair in their sixties.

I was in Austin, Texas and walking up the steps to the entrance of the old Confederate Home, which was constructed for use as a Confederate veterans' domicile.

The Texas Confederate Home was first established as a project of the John B. Hood Camp of United Confederate Veterans in 1884 in Clarksville, Texas. The Camp's main purpose was to establish a home for disabled and indigent Confederate veterans. In 1891 the Camp deeded the property on 26 acres of land on West 6th Street in Austin to the State. The complex included a large administration building and living quarters, a brick hospital, and private cottages. The name became officially Texas Confederate Home. After the last Confederate died in 1954, the act of the 48th legislature transferred "senile" mental patients from other State Hospitals to the Home.

As I entered the building I felt as if I were walking back into the 19th century. Everything looked gray, the exterior stone, the interior walls; the floors were dark, lending a shadowy appearance to the reception area.

The furnishings were uninviting, the shabby wooden chairs foretelling meager and minimal conditions for the inhabitants who were nowhere to be seen.

I was escorted by Louis DeMoll, Chief Social Worker, from the Central Office, the administrative Department, and the overseeing division of the State Mental Health Mental Retardation System. I had been associated with him several years before when he was consultant to my work on a community mental health center project in Wichita Falls, Texas. It was then that he suggested I enter the field of psychiatric social work.

Now as my supervisor at Confederate Home he was introducing me to the Superintendent and Medical Director, the only two full time physicians in this institution housing 600 male geriatric patients.

All had been transferred from the other State Mental Hospitals, Austin, San Antonio, Wichita Falls, Terrell and Rusk, when it was decided they required only custodial care. The average age of these men was 63; the average length of stay 18 years. Their diagnoses were manic depressive, various forms of Schizophrenia, and various forms of dementia. They were ordered to be transferred when they were considered to be unable to make use of any further treatment and designated as chronic. They were also believed to be without family resources and other living arrangements, earning them a lifetime of state supported custodial care. The family members were thought to be either non-existent, unable, or unwilling to care for the patient. The prevalent belief was that family members had lost interest and concern for the patient long ago. In a few months this hospital would be formally annexed by the Austin State Hospital, but the programs and treatment would be the same as before.

This hospital unlike the other state hospitals had no social service department, the functions of which in all other hospitals are to serve as liaison between the hospital on behalf of the patient and the family. The department's professionals are assigned to discharge planning for future placement. The absence of such a service prior to my employment implied the absence for the need of such services based on the philosophy of the custodial care hospital. Nothing was available to the patient outside of the hospital as well as any potential for employment in the outside world. The dire implication was that patients could not be expected to change.

The two physicians, elderly themselves, were cordial but looked disconcerted, even startled, and had little to say to this woman who literally had been thrust among them by institutional powers above. They were not sure how to receive me and not clear about the purpose of my presence there.

Indeed, why was I there? I who had started life over in my early 40's, having left my home and the profession of geology to enter the University of Texas School of Social Work, with the intention of specializing in what I felt was my calling, family psychotherapy, a relatively new field.

But first I intended to stop, rest, play, contemplate, and take time to decide on this crucial professional decision, especially at my age. There was a shortage in my profession and numerous job opportunities, some offering good salaries. However I wanted to think, take my time for the first time in years. I found myself wandering, drinking coffee with friends, and refinishing furniture for my apartment.

Taking responsibility for looking after my Mother and visiting her regularly, I began to think about her age group, the middle 70's. This was the one group I had not experienced professionally. They should be included in work with the family. I thought about her situation, a widow for 12 years, taking care of herself in a new town in a new state, Texas, learning to do things she had never done before, helping with her invalid brother, driving in the metropolitan city of Dallas, taking care of a large apartment, cooking, gardening and her own financial responsibilities, including investments.

My Father taught me what working for a living means to a man: a reason for living, repeating often that it was important for a man to like his work.

When I was 5 years old he took me downtown to see his office in downtown Atlanta. He admired his staff and treated them like family. He pointed out all the objects on his desk and their use. He gave me a pen and a notebook and a brand new company product, a Lily cup. I realized that he was proud of his job and everything connected to it. Before we left the office, he introduced me to his staff, citing their positions.

One of my prized possessions was an old Underwood typewriter from his office, a present for my eleventh birthday.

Two years later he was transferred to Mobile, Alabama as sales manager at the new Kraft Paper Mill. He took me and my brothers Lee, and Frank to the Mill to observe the process of making paper from pulp. He introduced us to the president of the company and the staff members in his department.

He was proud of the accomplishments of his company and usually discussed some interesting happening of the day at the dinner hour. At our house everyone was expected to join in. The children spoke first telling about the day at school. Then the grownups followed with my Father speaking last.

On one occasion he announced he had something of significance to tell after dinner. We were in suspense during the meal. Was it a promotion? A promised fishing trip on the company boat? Was it another transfer?

Everyone rushed through their experiences of the day to hear the promised story. At last he was ready.

"Children," he said speaking solemnly, "we have a new product, the very first of its kind to be used in Mobile, a white Kraft paper bag!"

I thought about my Grandfather, a difficult man in some respects, a German immigrant of the 19th century, hot tempered and authoritarian and not known for getting along with his superiors in the workplace. But he was very talented. He had worked for Levi Strauss, and he was a superb tailor. Mother considered him a genius at carpentering. He built a modern chicken house for his 200 chickens. And he built me a house when I was eleven. Not a doll house – a house. My younger brothers were involved in sports. I was a reader, also play acting on the stage. He thought I should have a house to entertain my friends. The doors were regular size, as were the four windows. A concrete porch with railing, two steps at one end of the porch, a tall pitched roof, shingled, bespoke a real house. I called it "the little house." My Grandfather was 75 when he built it. I learned from him what an old man can dream and do.

I knew the age group I would choose to work with now and this institution of unknown challenges and opportunities would be my first real job. I was sure what I would learn here would be important now and in the future for my work as a psychotherapist. As it turned out, it was important for my personal life as well. It was a fortuitous preparation for my life as I aged.

I learned months after coming to this position which was created for me, Chief Social Worker, that the hospital administration authority were not interested in developing a rehabilitation program. Unknown to me at the time was the fact that I was hired as a social worker who would develop a program of discharge for patients to nursing homes and other suitable institutions with the goal of closing the hospital. I was excited as I set my goals: to offer rehabilitative changes designed for the individual patient and to make contact with as many of the families of the 600 patients as possible.

Subchapter 11a – The Introduction

I was escorted by the Medical Director to a narrow stairway leading to the upstairs room selected to be my office. A large square featureless room with ceiling that seemed to end in the stratosphere was interrupted by two very narrow very high windows, I judged 12 feet. The plastered walls were, as we used to say, "dead white." There was a desk and chair with the severe lines of the ones downstairs. The Director told me he had put a buzzer under the desk drawer for me to summon help in the event of an attack by a violent patient. I told him I didn't think I would need it, and he became agitated and reminded me, "Mrs. Moon, these are mental patients."

He was a tall thin man appearing to be in his late sixties with anxious looking eyes and whose frame and limbs seemed to move in all directions.

I asked permission to decorate the room a bit and he told me graciously to help myself to the furnishings in the basement. These were left over from years when women, presumably relatives of the veterans, assisted with trying to provide a more homelike atmosphere.

I was surprised to find colorful orange yellow and green foliage-printed upholstery, a white wicker set, and drapes, to match the upholstery. Since they were ridiculously short as drapes they served nicely as valances. I put large green potted plants in two corners and a small one on the desk. I found a green rug for the worn dark oak floor. Now I could relax and work in this room and try to figure out how to be of use to these men.

The surprise continued. I was given a secretary. She was a pretty brunette 19 years old, appearing very mature for her age, and certainly with none of the Hippie tags about her. She was a second year psychology student majoring in the social sciences and a talented artist. My mind was full of all the ways she could apply her gifts. She was enthusiastic and eager to be involved in what I described as an adventure and an opportunity to achieve something novel and exciting.

We then went to visit the wards, large gray-walled spaces with tall barred windows. There were few attendants in each ward. The staff were generally middle-aged or elderly, all dressed in white shirts and trousers, looking very much like the patients, except for the khaki clothes worn by the patients.

I was met by the one registered nurse, the director of nurses, a plump, pleasant faced woman in her 50's, who greeted me with a professional, reserved smile. I stated that I recognized her authority and let her know by my nod to her rank that I had no intention to interfere with her regimen.

Patients milled about or sat at table games or listened to the radio. There was a workshop of sorts, and a smaller room where patients could draw on paper with pencils or crayons.

Soon after my arrival, several patients were transferred from the San Antonio State Hospital and immediately herded into a room called the "lockup" awaiting inspection by the nurse and attendants. There was nothing in the way of an orientation to ease the anxiety of transfer to a strange place and no formal introductions. I was horrified at what I saw as the staff not understanding how patients would feel – frightened and disturbed at such treatment, not cruel, certainly, but unconcerned and without compassion. Though there was no intent to do harm, it was unconsciously uncaring.

So here is where I would begin, with a new kind of beginning for the patients. I told the nurse I would appreciate being able to give an orientation to our department in the form of a get-together with the patients and staff selected by the nurse, and of course including herself as well as the staff dentist, whom I had just met, a likeable fellow with a sense of humor. That was apparent when he greeted me with a wink and said he too was "new here" and glad to meet another "fellow member."

I asked for a smaller room for more intimacy and a cart to be brought in with coffee and cookies. The attendants looked questioningly at each other and glanced sideways at the nurse to see her reaction. The nurse looked startled for a moment, being caught off guard, but she must have realized I had carte blanche from the superintendent and agreed to my request.

That afternoon we met in one of the smaller wards, and I asked all to sit in a circle. They moved uneasily as if they had never done this before, and indeed they had not. I introduced myself and my secretary and told them we had come to meet the patients, welcome them to the hospital and find out more about them, so we could plan some interesting things for them to do. The secretary and I told them about our interests and what we liked to do and asked each person in the group to do the same. We took turns starting with the nurse, who had no difficulty entering into the program. When the patients hesitated, I asked them where they were from, what had been their home. I wanted to know what hobbies they enjoyed and what hospital activities they liked.

No one spoke up spontaneously. We could act as if this activity were the most usual and normal thing in the world, but we knew that this experience if known by the patients had long been forgotten. While not responding verbally, all were attentive and very much present.

I believed the message had been received by staff and patients: social service was here to help with the transition to this hospital, help them understand and cope with what was happening to them, and know that we cared about who they were, what they thought, and would help them find something interesting to do. The staff understood I was not interfering with the medical regimen, even though I was surely interfering with the regimentation of persons and the ignoring of human feelings. At the close of this unsophisticated first group session, the patients seemed more relaxed and were smiling, and the refreshments brought on more communication among staff and patients. I wondered if this simple universal social event might reach into the memories of the patients. I was relieved when the nurse said, "This was a good idea and went better than I thought." Again I observed the low expectations on the part of staff in regard to patients' behavior. I was not concerned about the minimal participation because I saw that each had taken a step toward communicative involvement. I thanked the nurse for her direction and participation as well as the attendants' cooperation. I felt I had made friends with the staff and I was "in."

The next day I began my visits with the patients on their wards, 20 or more each day. Part of each day was devoted by me and the secretary to examining the charts. Each patient chart was several inches thick, reflecting years of medical recording. Each had been in one or more mental hospitals previously. We would make a 5 X 8 index card for each man, documenting the salient information: age, diagnosis, past treatment, date first hospitalized, family names, residence, education level, work experience, talents, interests, hobbies. The purpose and goal of my program was social and emotional rehabilitation. What it would take to achieve this we would discover as we talked and worked with the patient in order to guide him to a more satisfying and functioning self.

Rehabilitation to me meant the resurrection and revival of interests and capabilities, which would be the basis for helping him to lead a more normal, fuller, enjoyable life. I am indebted in this way of thinking to a gift of a fellowship stipend from the Office of Vocational Rehabilitation when I was a first year graduate social work student. The only requirement was that I "become interested in the concept of vocational rehabilitation." I attended several workshops under their auspices and found the physiological concepts to be relevant and valuable and transferrable in working with all mental patients in this setting and with working with patients and families in the future.

There were 600 charts to be examined. We read as many as possible each day, working through lunch time, and made our card file. We had an additional card for each in which we recorded the most significant data from our contacts with the patient. The work was tedious but the discovery of unexpected, fascinating information was worth it.

The decades of medical records had more than enough of the patients' weaknesses. My goal was to catalogue and document their strengths on which a plan for whatever rehabilitation was possible could be built.

Subchapter 11b – The Play's the Thing

In our visits with the patients we observed that the attendants often didn't understand what we were trying to accomplish and even thought our communication and work with the patients were strange. From their point of view, they would say this, that we were wasting our time trying to effect change in patients. We had succeeded with the plan for orienting patients on admission to the hospital, now we realized we needed to design a plan for training staff to become oriented to our treatment methods.

The value of visual aids had been known for a long time now but I had learned even more the value of dramatic presentation as a communication and teaching tool as a Paleontology instructor 16 years before: "The play's the thing by which we catch the conscience of the king."

The next step in our program was to put on a show for the staff, all three shifts.

The director of nurses, the dentist, the secretary and I met over coffee and I suggested the play. The title would be "Confederate Home: past and present." My idea was to portray the hospital with its present undesirable practices and orientation to patient care but call it "past." Then to present and act our desirable and remedial hoped for practices and call them "present." The reason for this was to present a positive rather than a negative critical portrayal. When an actor as an attendant would demonstrate harsh and disrespectful behavior, we would say this was the old way in the old days. Then the present portrayal would illustrate a corrective mode of behavior. The first act would be the "Past," the second the "Present" as corrective. I knew it was corny, but it worked, because it would get the message over to the attendant without finger pointing and intimidating but demonstrate how hurtful negative behavior on the part of the staff influenced patients negatively.

What made it work was that it was interesting for the staff audience to watch and everyone who chose to would have a chance to be in the show. The audience, i.e., the next performers would have "seen the show" and have an advantage in acting the parts. An attendant could select his part and improvise the script accordingly. The first act would be performed by the nurse, the dentist, who played a patient, the secretary as the social worker, two attendants who were brave enough to go on first, and I would be the moderator and narrator of the prologue and the epilogue.

It was interesting that the two attendants wanted to be the bad guys. The dentist should have won an Academy Award for his portrayal of a patient. He suggested that he behave disorderly and have the attendant crack a whip over his head. It was cruel and unusual punishment of the kind that didn't happen actually. They loved it and several wanted to volunteer for the part.

When the show for the first shift was over, and after the epilogue and bows, I called on the attendants in the viewing audience to play the parts for the succeeding shift, and they in turn would do likewise for the last shift. The members of the audience, seeing their peers perform in the first production realized they could also act the parts. Some even had suggestions for additions to the scenes, with additional bad or good behaviors to be enacted. As soon as the announcement "Curtain!" was heard hands went up all over the house to volunteer.

The two physicians, the Superintendent and the Medical Director attended, standing but looking at each other from time to time. They were open-mouthed as the "audience" applauded loudly at the end of the performance. They departed quietly to their offices, so I'm not sure what they made of it, but I believe the staff got the point of the picture, enjoyed their participation and learned from it. The nurse beamed, shook my hand, and became a real friend.

Meanwhile reading and study of the charts continued daily. One of the most interesting discoveries was the work history of many patients. Here was a basis for encouraging revival of their skills. I was startled one day to see that some patients had previously received Social Security payments, and others became eligible during hospitalization but had not received this information, so had not applied for their allotment. I called the local Social Security representative, and she assured me the situation would be rectified. It was rewarding for us to know that these patients who thought they had no money would now receive Social Security payments.

Of course there were some who had no financial resources. I approached the Central Office Medical Director, telling him my concerns about them. He was unimpressed, "After all their needs are being taken care of." I asked him how he would feel about himself as a man, knowing that he didn't have a nickel in his pocket to buy a coke. He frowned then he said, grinding his teeth, "Well, when you put it that way." Then he said he would see to some allowances.

There was one other very important ongoing project: contacting the families. We wrote letters to the known family members and distant relatives. Thanks to my secretary who was a talented cartoonist, the pink, yellow, and green notes were illustrated representing some idea or situation involving the patient. I decided on that great communicant, the dog to do what he does best, send a universal message in a humorous childlike way, as a patient of course.

So here was the little dog on the cover writing to his dear family, then turning inside he would be seen atop his house, musing about some recent incident, or writing at his desk about his feelings, or sitting alone on a hospital bench. The message might reflect his feelings of homesickness for his family, or happiness at some achievement, wishing for something material from his folks, or merely philosophizing about his life at Confederate Home.

Having spent so much of my adolescent years on the amateur stage, I thought it only natural to use fantasy and characters to tell a story. And of course the dog was my favorite character, having been a dog owner since childhood. At the end of the year, believing that we must have built up a relationship between us and the families through our letters, we decided it was time to bring them in person as a group to the hospital. All family contacts would be invited. What better way than a grand picnic on the grounds! We wrote "there will be lunch, dessert, and iced tea for all. We'll have fun, so please come." We didn't require RSVP, thinking such a commitment from them might make them hesitate. We wanted to send the message that we would be receiving company, no matter how many, with refreshments for all. We had to guess at the number. I told the superintendent to plan for at least 200 based on the meager information in the records.

On the morning of the event an orderly reported that the superintendent had arranged for 4 tables and 8 benches. The picnic was set for noon.

Shortly after daylight the attendants came running to say the caravan was arriving. When I arrived at the hospital at 7:00 we could see them in the distance coming over the hill by car, truck and horse and wagon – over 300 strong. The superintendent, frantic, called the city recreation department to send all the available tables and benches. The kitchen hastily added more to the store of food. I believe there was enough, and of course the families, used to the celebration of a picnic on the grounds arrived bearing a great feast.

We learned from some of the families that they were not aware that visiting the patient was possible or that they could be permitted to take the patient home if they were able to care for him. Some had not written for years and were thrilled with the opportunity afforded this day to visit in the future or take the patient home.

It was a glorious day and a glorious ending to our rehabilitation program. It was a glorious beginning for many of the patients and their families and one more lesson for the staff.

And so it was for me. The knowledge I had gained from the results of my program would serve as a basis for the work in many future psychiatric settings. The knowledge gained from these chronic patients, discovering their capabilities for growth and change gave me the confidence to engage with many other types of patients and situations considered hopeless.

Subchapter 11c – The Depression Teacher

The patient was sitting on a narrow wooden bench in the hall, arms hanging at his side. I stopped and greeted him,

"Good morning, Mr. Perry."

He did not respond. I don't believe in pushing, so I told him I would see him later and went to research his chart further for information about depression. "Manic depressive," the nurse said as she handed me the chart which was three inches thick, the edges of the pages ragged from so much handling over the 9 years of hospitalization.

I met Mr. Perry soon after I began work at the Confederate Home, my first appointment after graduation. This experience was also to serve as qualifying for my certification as psychiatric social worker.

Most of the data about Mr. Perry reflected administering of medications, changing doses on disturbing behavior and changing diagnoses. The chart could have belonged to dozens of other patients. It took some time to find the person tucked away in those pages. The chief medical officer indulged me, the message sent me from above was: "Go ahead, see if she can help him, probably can't – but probably won't hurt."

I was not a medical technician, of course, but a psychotherapist whose goal was emotional and social rehabilitation, enabling the patient to begin a path toward rewarding and self-sufficient living. This was a hospital comprising 600 men, average age 63, with an average hospital stay of 18 years. An unofficial word used among the professionals to describe this type of hospitalization was warehousing.

The treatment was perfunctory: medications with little personal attention, the reason being that the chronically ill psychiatric patient, particularly the elderly, were considered to be "incapable of making use of any kind of therapy."

You may wonder why I chose such a hospital. It was here I would test my theories about helping people to change. I was often considered odd, at the very least naïve because I had faith in the importance of the role of relationship in work with psychiatric patients and a belief in the mental powers of the elderly.

I was in my early forties, but I had learned about the remarkable abilities of the elderly, from my parents, my grandfather, my great-aunts, and friends.

Sherds – a Mémoire

The year was 1963 before much had been written about the accomplishments of psychiatric treatment with elderly patients. I was told later the mission of the administration was to evacuate the hospital and discharge patients to nursing homes. I also learned much later that I was certainly not hired as a therapist to promote change in patients, but to officiate in their discharge to nursing facilities. This was the environment I had to work with, although I did not know it at the time, or that my one year there would be all the time I would be given to do my work. Thanks to a brilliant and compassionate supervisor who interceded for and supported me I was given leeway to pursue many innovative programs.

Reading Mr. Perry's chart I found a high school education. He was raised on a farm, and had worked in a local feed store. He was from a family whose members were well known for their accomplishments. I thought his appearance reflected a handsome man in former years. The history provided the information that he had managed his farm sufficiently until his wife died and financial reverses occurred. He then experienced a depressive episode, and there being no other resources, he was sent to the nearest state hospital which was at Terrell near Dallas. There the patients were allowed to work in the vegetable garden. Mr. Perry's talents surfaced and he no longer exhibited depression.

Later for some reason not discernable in the chart he was transferred to this hospital where there was no gardening program. The record then stated simply the "patient became depressed for no reason." I didn't think it took a psychotherapist to regard this as not making common sense. I was to learn this was all too ready an explanation for men exhibiting depression. What the chart didn't say but implied was that their depression was a mystery.

Finally Mr. Perry was returned to Terrell where he resumed his work in the garden. A brief note declared, "He no longer exhibited depression."

When I met him he had just been returned to Austin. I thought I knew a technique to assist in helping people, one which would provide a bridge to communication and something meaningful to this person. I had neglected to water the plant on my desk and it was badly wilted. It looked certainly beyond my help, so I brought it with me on my second approach to my patient. I greeted him and told him that I understood he was knowledgeable about plants and asked him if he could help me with this one. This time he raised his head – and I thought – in the manner of a flower after being watered. He looked at me and answered that he could.

I found more such projects for him to work on and he showed interest and animation and no signs of depression. I recorded his activities in the chart and on my file cards.

After a few weeks I petitioned my supervisor to allow Mr. Perry to come to my house, a one-acre place on the edge of town. The present project was a large herb garden begun by the former owner, a horticulturist, but languishing under my attentions. In a few weeks the garden was revived, had been enlarged in size, and was thriving. He then set out 80 tomato plants and vegetables of many varieties, including a large stand of corn, green peppers, and cantaloupes. The harvest produced enough to furnish my Mother's canning arts, and share with the neighbors, who also raised vegetable and fruits on their 5 and 10 acre tracts. Mr. Perry was happy, and this experience for me was the fulfillment of my earliest fantasies – living as if in a small agrarian community.

At the end of the year the hospital was ordered closed, and the patients who had benefited from rehabilitation were allowed to be discharged to suitable semi-independent living situations. There was no farm environment available to Mr. Perry. When I told him he was qualified to be discharged to a goat ranch he was not happy about the opportunity and became depressed again.

I scheduled several sessions with him to talk over the proposed change. I asked what it was he liked about working with plants, and he said "It was being outdoors and making things grow." I asked him if he could think about transferring these interests to the situation on a goat ranch. There he would be outside as he liked. I told him I believed he was capable of change, had a good mind, was creative, and therefore would be able to adapt to this situation. He said, "But you won't be there."

I told him that would happen in any case with the hospital closing, but that he would always have the memory of our work together and of our relationship which he could use in making friends with others. He was reluctant, but he finally agreed to the change. I told him I thought it would be much better than a hospital. I hoped he would remember that.

Now 44 years later when I read about the current theories and the medical methods for depression Mr. Perry always comes to mind.

Subchapter 11d – The Courtly Mr. Courtley

A tall dignified gray haired man, a patient at the Confederate Home approached me as I was making my rounds one fall morning. I had not met him before. He appeared very different from the patients I knew. He held himself erect as he walked straight toward me. He came directly to the point.

"My name is Courtley. I hear you are the new social worker. I'd like an appointment with you. I'm ready to go home."

He was the first patient to introduce himself to me, to state his name on meeting, to use the word appointment to even know the name of my position, social worker. Patients were not routinely discharged from this hospital before I came. There was no system for discharge, because there was no social service department for such execution. From his language I supposed he was someone who was educated and sure of himself, characteristics very different from the patients I had met. I told him I would call the Medical Director for permission to set up an appointment.

The Medical Director, a recent refugee from Cuba, usually a calm and mild-mannered man, blurted out in a high voice to my request,

"But Mrs. Moon, the man is crazy. He came to me saying he must see you, even demanding to leave."

Before I could respond he continued.

"Did you know he says he is a millionaire? That he lives in a mansion and that he is the cousin of the Mexican consul?"

"It's true, Dr. Alera," I answered.

But he says he owns a mansion on two acres in downtown Dallas.

"So he does, Dr. Alera."

"He says he has a Chrysler which he personally has engineered the air conditioning. And he repeated, stuttering now, he says his cousin is the Consul to Mexico."

"All true, Doctor."

"So why is he in the hospital?"

"Why indeed, Doctor?"

The physician answered with a last question, almost sadly,

"Why do you say these things, Mrs. Moon?"

I told him the first clue I had came from his medical record. Five years ago he was a patient at Timberlawn Sanitarium, a private psychiatric hospital, whose admittants had to be wealthy, the fee was several thousand a month. As a student I had attended seminars there and was well acquainted with the place.

Further I had studied Mr. Courtley's chart and the facts therein substantiated his claims. I promised to examine the details of his admission and discharges to find out why he was discharged from the other hospitals after Timberlawn and why he wound up here after 5 years.

I arranged an appointment with Mr. Courtley and we met in my office. He exhibited a high level of anxiety, very similar to the kind of frenetic impatience I had observed in the past with businessmen who were head of companies and had little tolerance for suffering incompetence. Such men became annoyed with people they thought were not showing them the proper respect. Apparently from some examples Mr. Courtley mentioned, his impatience turned to anger then to obstreperous behavior, like throwing things and shouting at staff, and when penalties failed to subdue him, they discharged him.

His chart described an initial period of depression following the death of his wife, which was then followed by a mild stroke, for which he was hospitalized at Timberlawn. It is well known that behavioral problems often occur in personalities like his, particularly after a stroke. His behavior became increasingly demanding until he was found "unsuitable for therapy" and discharged to the nearby state hospital at Terrell.

While there, the record shows that his behavior was considered to be "unreasonable" and did not improve, and "since he was 66 years old," he was transferred to the Confederate Home, the hospital for elderly chronic patients.

I realized I was offered a limited amount of time to work with Mr. Courtley, and in view of his personality, I decided to work with a cognitive-behavioral approach, common sense, down to earth.

In effect my message and hence my goal would be to communicate "Now look, you know what it takes to get out and go home, don't you, and are you then willing to do what it takes to get there?" Now, of course, I did not use these exact words. I was formal but matter of fact. I pointed out that I understood his frustration at not being treated with the respect he deserved but that his responses were a hindrance to achieving his goal, namely returning home to his living as he wished. I reassured him that I knew he was capable of coping with the present situation and had the strength and intelligence to do so. I guessed he had never been in a position to give in to others before his hospitalizations. He seemed relieved.

"Finally someone understands my situation."

The Medical Director had to be reassured that before Mr. Courtley could return home, there must be proof that his home situation was in order. I suggested one of my favorite methods of the social worker – a home visit. Now a home visit was a new concept to the Director, let alone a visit 200 miles away. However by now the administration was getting used to the unusual aspects of my approach and granted permission for the day trip to Dallas. The stipulation was that a ward attendant accompany us.

The attendant, the patient, and I drove in my car and arrived early in the day. Mr. Courtley's memory of directions through the city and to his home was unimpaired. The large gray stone house on a high hill was visible a mile before we reached the sprawling lawn with abundant shrubbery and flowers. Stepping out of the car and standing in the midst of his crepe myrtles and azaleas, he pointed out the names of the varieties.

"Let me show you a good view of the city," he said. He gestured from the highest point of the hill where we stood, on two lovely acres close to the downtown of Dallas. The attendant uttered only, "Oh, my!" as we made our way through the grounds to the house.

He proudly guided us through his spacious home, describing the mahogany and walnut Empire period furniture, elegant but not ostentatious, as we went from room to room. He moved easily and unconcerned as if he had never been away. We went outside again to see his car in the garage, and he beamed pointing out its features as if he were showing it for the first time.

"Notice the leather interior, I've attended to its maintenance – in the past, of course," he acknowledged smiling. As we prepared to go back to Austin I noticed that Mr. Courtley did not hesitate. He was willing to return, apparently feeling all was well. He looked relaxed and happy.

"You'll be back soon," I promised.

It was only a week later when the limousine drove up to the hospital yard. The consul and his wife, he in a dark suit and she in a light blue silk one trimmed in fur, stepped smiling from the limousine. They shook hands with the Medical Director who officiated and smiled broadly, while a group of the patients gathered round a respectful distance and waived. The family and patient left amid loud good wishes and good byes. It had all been great fun.

Thanks to Mr. Courtley I had learned in fact what I had been taught – the supreme importance of the medical record as a tool of treatment rather than a mere repository of facts. From this experience I learned particularly the value of the therapist as sleuth in the discovery of a trove of data, which points like a compass to the direction and activity of the therapy.

In addition this was the first time I thought of my diagnosis and therapy as a romp. I am obligated to this patient for supplying me with the substance and opportunity to use myself in a humorous way to promote a therapeutic outcome. It wasn't that I was ostensibly funny on the outside as much as I was enjoying and employing the comic irony on the inside as I worked. I decided to ply humor actively in the future work in the hospital because I could see the humor in every aspect of the hospital procedures, and a place for it at appropriate times in the therapy.

I had already planned dramatic presentations in order to orient staff to more humane methods and send messages to the families in the form of cartoons. This was a way to bring some levity to the heavy load of staff and to the tragic circumstance of the patients. Some would think I had a strange goal: to bring enjoyment to therapy. I had learned and would continue to find that it was a necessary component.

Subchapter 11e – The Mechanic

In my continuing research of the hospital charts to seek out patients with talents, skills, and prior work experience I discovered Mr. Johnson. He was a transfer like all the others from another state hospital to the Confederate Home, in this case from Terrell. The reason for his transfer was his obsessive compulsive behavior which interfered with continuing treatment. After a lengthy period of the treatment offered it was decided that he could no longer make use of treatment. The result was transfer to what amounted to custodial care.

I knew from experience that people with this diagnosis were extremely rigid personalities and very resistant to developing relationships with their therapists and most kinds of treatment. So Mr. Johnson promised to be a very difficult project for me. However I was encouraged by one interesting statement in the medical record. He had been a mechanic for many years at the Ford Motor Company in Dallas, and from other comments in the history had been very competent. After all my focus was on rehabilitation to whatever extent possible, so I sought him out.

I was directed to the hospital workshop where I found him, a man of 63, medium build, hat pulled down almost to his eyes, looking intently ahead as he worked at the weaver's loom. He was weaving a brightly colored rug. I called him by name and introduced myself. No answer. I asked if I might look at his work. He stopped but did not look at me as I continuing talking about what I saw. He finally asked if I knew anything about weaving. I said, "not a thing." I was always glad to let a patient know he knew more than I did. He then set out to describe the loom, all its parts, detailing the dimensions, the kind of wood, where the wood came from when he started building it, the problems with building, and so on.

"Building it?" I interrupted – you have to interrupt an obsessive compulsive personality if you're going to have a conversation instead of a monologue. I then stepped back, should he become angry at the interruption. He did raise his voice very loudly, answering, "Yes, I built it." "How wonderful!" I said, glancing at my watch as he continued, "I discovered the movement of weaving is just like the movement in the pistons of an engine, so I designed it. I made a lot of rugs for the hospital." I imagined he made quite a number in his 15 years in this hospital.

I told him I was here to help people start life again outside of the hospital and to return home if possible and also find employment.

He said quickly that's what he wanted, but the hospital wouldn't let him go home. I suggested that we take one step at a time and start by talking in my office; making a plan for the future. He said, "I'm not good at talking," but agreed to meeting me at the office.

From the beginning we had a communication problem at every level. He wanted to go home to his wife, but I found out that his wife had divorced him years ago. I was not sure whether he had not been told or whether he had not accepted it. I guessed it was the latter, although it was not unusual for staff to withhold such information from the patient, so as not to disturb them further. We did not speak the same language. I could see he was going to test my ability to communicate.

His language was not only colloquial but abstruse and repetitious.

But here was the opportunity because he was obviously intelligent and he liked to work, important assets for his rehabilitation.
So I began with the subject introduced by him, his wife.

"Tell me about her," I said.

He described her physically, "Dark hair and eyes, small, not strong." Period.

Taking my cue from "not strong" I asked, grateful to be able to follow his lead, "Was she sick?"

"No – couldn't lift furniture."

I was sure there in lay a story, but pursuing this led only to "Well, just couldn't lift furniture."

I wanted to know about her personality.

"Yes she had one." What kind of led only to vigorous rubbing of his hands.

Now the important question, "How did you get along?"

"All right."

"Were there any difficulties between you?"

A blank stare.

"Were there any problems."

"No, I'm good at arithmetic."

"Were there any stresses..." I went on to use every synonym at my disposal. The answer was always the same,

"No, nothing, no."

I reached for the last of my wits, "Did you ever have any fusses?"

"Oh, yeah, all the time."

I am indebted to Mr. Johnson for helping me learn never to take my own communication for granted.

So then instead of being able to discuss issues of difference between them, he continued on about having to go to the hospital instead of going home.

"But now," he said, "I like my weaver's job. I need to work," he repeated over and over.

I decided this is where I would concentrate my emphasis.

"But no, I want to go home to my wife. It'll be all right," he insisted. The job issue would have to wait.

I took the next step, I called his wife. Yes, they were divorced, she would be willing to talk with me but could not face coming to the hospital for a meeting, even with me as mediator.

I asked the superintendent for permission to talk with her in Dallas, so that I could obtain information in order to help him. I assured her there would be no pressure to persuade her to do anything.

Fortunately I obtained the permission to make another home visit. The superintendent let me know that he did not expect the trip to produce anything of value. Such predictions were always ready and simple based on their knowledge and experience. I told him I hoped something constructive would develop from the visit for both parties.

I drove to Dallas alone. Mrs. Johnson came to the door after my first ring. She was a pretty woman in her fifties, neat and trim and a little smile with eyes searching mine expectantly. The house was small, tastefully but sparsely furnished with two pictures on the wall. Colors were monotone, grays and blues blended. The somber seascapes seem to set the tone for the décor. Mrs. Johnson had coffee ready for the coffee table.

She expressed her concern right away, "I feel sorry for him, but I have never been able to help him, I could never please him."

"I cannot have him return home," she said sadly but firmly. She divorced him years ago but felt too guilty all these years to allow herself to marry someone else she had known and loved for a long time.

She cried, "Then, no one understood – my husband would not accept help and I couldn't help him, but I have no need to hurt him." To her divorce was terrible and the source of her guilt feelings.

She reinforced her reluctance to be with him again, stating, "It was his temper. He never harmed me, but discussion of problems only led to outbursts of temper."

She repeated, "He never harmed me. He wasn't a bad man."

Finally I asked if she thought she had a right to live her own life now after so long a time? Did she think she should continue to carry such a burden of guilt that prevented her from living in peace?

I told her Mr. Johnson was being taken care of, and I believed he could make it alone, as he seemed to be doing now.

When it came time for me to leave she took my hand and said, "I'm glad you came. You did help me with what I've been hoping for but I felt I could never have peace of mind to live my own life."

I returned to the hospital and went to the workshop thinking this setting would be easier for both of us to talk about my visit with his wife. I told him we had a good visit. His first words were, "Yes, I knew you would."

He emphasized the word "you." In the past others had said they would try to talk with his wife but apparently had felt too embarrassed to do so.

Although Mr. Johnson still didn't look at me when he spoke, he appeared quieter and more at ease.

I asked if he would like to ask any questions about my visit with his wife.

He shook his head, "I think I knew... She got a divorce, didn't she? Is she all right?"

I said, "Yes, she's all right, and she wants you to be happy."

He ran his fingers back and forth on the wood of the loom and didn't say anything for a long time. I sat there while he worked the loom, waiting until he spoke, then he turned and looked at me and said, "That's good."

Subchapter 11f – The Cook

Mr. Brown was one of the more fortunate patients at the Confederate Home for chronic psychiatric and geriatric patients. He had a job. So to speak. He worked daily for a few hours in the hospital canteen serving soft drinks and packaged snacks. He earned, besides his daily allotment of cigarettes doled out to him by his attendant supervisor, a quarter a week.

I discovered him as I did most of the patients by searching through the charts for individuals most likely qualified for therapy and discharge to semi-independent living. The criteria consisted of the patient's present functioning as well as abilities and talents referred to in the past. Hearing of other patients having been interviewed by me he sent a request through a friendly ward attendant. He wanted to go to Waco to see his wife.

Before meeting with him I reviewed more carefully the ten years of notes in order to be more specific as I set up the treatment plan. I was shocked to discover his wife had died some years before but he had not been told. I asked the attendant who referred him how this could happen? "We tried to tell him, but it was just too hard, so I guess we just dropped it and then forgot all about it."

Then he added, "Besides we knew he would just get upset, and we try to keep them quiet."

My goal would be to tell him the truth, help him through the grief process, and then plan with him for some kind of job. He had an undeniable strength – he formerly had been a cook in a café.

I went directly to the canteen to meet with him and to tell him I would set up an appointment to talk with him about his prospects. He was 62 years old and his somewhat round face showed the kind of resignation at the acceptance of his circumstances typical of the patients here. His clothing seemed a part of the drab ward décor, I wondered if he ever thought about it: the brown baggy pants turned up poorly at the cuff, the grey-green shirt, surely unironed, the shoes so worn it was hard to tell the color. The bright spot in the aspect were his eyes, large and dark and open wide and shining – I guessed with hope – and looking wonderingly as I began to talk about our interview.

The canteen supervisor, Mrs. James, stood beside him, half blocking his body as she asked what I wanted. She was a tall thin woman with dark squinting eyes and lips pressed into a firm straight line.

"He's my patient," she said without hesitation. "He works for me. He doesn't have any time to be off."

"Works for her indeed," I thought. That's a switch. Had anyone ever told them staff is supposed to work for patients? I was to learn every day that this philosophy had not made its way to this environment.

In 1963 the movement to emphasize mental health instead of mental illness was abroad in the country, but the atmosphere here belonged to another era.

Not that the staff was intentionally cruel to the patients, merely fiercely paternalistic, as if the old men were not men but children to be cared for and told what to do.

Hearing the words of his supervisor, Mr. Brown turned his head away, bowed as if to his fate, and he held his hands tightly together. I wondered if he were trying to hold himself together.

I said good bye as cheerily as I was able under the glare of the supervisor's eyes, and told Mr. Brown I would be seeing him soon.

I went immediately to the superintendent's office. I would protest what I observed as the attendant standing between me and the patient. Dr. Parnell was calm and matter of fact as he said he did not "want to offend Mrs. James as she was a good employee and provided a needed service." I was naïve at being surprised that he was concerned about the feelings of the attendant rather than the patient.

I didn't argue further but made an appointment with my supervisor in the Central Office, the top division in the Department of Mental Health Mental Retardation State of Texas. Mr. DeMoll was a brilliant man, dedicated to the patient, possessing a gift for the words of diplomacy. He let me know that I should calm down and use my wits to get through this impasse. I was to receive his direction many times as I became excited trying to fight for the patients' rights, a concept as yet not familiar to the staff. I was not going to be able to restrain Mrs. James, but I did receive permission to work with the patient.

Mr. Brown showed up at my office the next day, cap in hand, stopping at the door to my office as if he needed permission to enter this atypical hospital room. He stood fixed when greeted, looking around my newly decorated office with ancient but highly colorful green, yellow, and orange upholstery, window drapes, and antique wicker furniture. His mouth dropped open and his eyes moved from side to side taking in the bright furnishings.

He sat down at my invitation, his eyes fixed on the things on my desk, the green plant and the pictures of loved ones. I told him he had good prospects for leaving the institution. "With your background as cook, it would be easy for you to find employment."

"I just worked in a café," he said, "Just one café."

"Well, for how long, Mr. Brown?"

"Eight years."

"My goodness, that's a good long time," I said with real enthusiasm.

I said that while his employment in the canteen offered some freedom from less interesting chores elsewhere in the hospital I let him know I gathered that his work with Mrs. James was not much fun.

He grinned at the prospect of "being free."

"I'll be glad to go home to my wife."

I asked if he wondered why he had not heard from her for years.

"Well, she never did write much."

There was no way out for me, I knew I had to tell him what I knew. Sooner or later he would learn the truth elsewhere though through what I knew would be a blunt message.

I told him as carefully and gently as I could that she had passed away, I did not say when.

He was quiet for a few minutes and then began to weep. I offered him a tissue. He looked up at me in surprise at my action. I had seen this reaction before from other patients. Ordinary assists with emotions in patients was not the custom among treatment people at that time.

He didn't ask any particulars, when she died or anything about the occurrence.

I asked if he ever thought she might have died?

"Yes, but I couldn't believe it. It was too hard."

Then he added, "after all I've been here a long time."

"A long time?" I repeated.

"Anything can happen when you're here a long time."

Since this suggested finality, and he did not want to talk further and had not answered questions about other issues that might have bothered him in the past, I did not pursue further.

He seemed relieved about his new view of the future and said, "I'd better get back now."

When I went to see him the next day he wasn't in the ward. The attendant said he'd been put in the lockup by Mrs. James.

The attendant enabled me to gain entry to the small cell with no difficulty. I sat down beside him on the cot and said, "Tell me what happened."

I presumed someone had notified Mrs. James of my presence in the lockup, because in a few minutes she came in and stood close, looking down at me.

"When he came back from seeing you," she said, "he was disturbed, laughing, and telling me he didn't have to go back to the canteen because he was leaving. I told him he couldn't go because he talked back to me, so I put him in the lockup."

With a sharp look to the attendant who admitted me to the cell she left in quick strides.

He sat looking dejected with his head in his hands. I asked him to talk with me about his feelings in the matter.

"She took away my cigarettes."

Actually the cigarettes were supplied by the hospital regularly to all patients requesting them. So I thought, he is being punished for being happy and expressing himself.

I calmed myself down as I had been instructed by my supervisor, but I went back to the superintendent again and asked permission to give the patient his cigarettes. The superintendent appeared perplexed at my request, but whether it was because of my persistence, the patient, or the actions of Mrs. James he gave orders to release the patient from the lockup.

This episode had set Mr. Brown back in his resolve to start a new life. My training had taught me to expect this regressive behavior in response to rebuke or disappointment. When I went back to talk with him on the ward, he greeted me with, "Things are not so bad, and I can work again at the canteen. I'll get my quarter and cigarettes and I have a table and a bed."

Withdrawal is to be expected when patients try to move forward and encounter obstacles, however I held on to the idea of what mattered most to him.

I said, "Yes, you have all these things, but wouldn't you like to have a hot plate? You could do a little cooking for yourself then."

That did it. He smiled and said dreamily, "A hot plate."

Several days later he was preparing to depart to a halfway house which had been located and he was given a two room apartment with a stove and refrigerator. He was also scheduled to take a part-time job in a nearby café.

I sat with him as we waited for a station wagon to pick him up. We discussed his duties as bus boy and also serving customers as well as helping with the cooking.

"I know how to do that," he said. I was relieved at his expression of confidence.

I described his new living quarters and what I knew about them.

"And I'll have a hot plate, won't I, Mrs. Moon?"

"You'll have a real stove, Mr. Brown, a real stove!"

Defectives

I had no knowledge then to care,
much less to find a time to spare
for such a hurting one as you
when I had so much else to do.

I've little space for house and run
you needed little, just someone
to take you in and learn somehow
to be the one you needed now.

You did not press upon my heart
but touched so slightly at the start
and in a while the place that you
made yours became my refuge too.

Chapter 12 – The Practice: The House on Ardath Street

It was the sixth year of my career as a family psychotherapist, employed in the office of a psychiatrist in Wichita Falls, Texas in 1968. We had known each other briefly some years before, and he knew only that I had completed five years of specialized training in my field. His specialty was treating patients with what he called "medical control," psychotropic drugs. He chose me to assist him because he recognized the need to associate with someone who would be available to patients who preferred to work on problems in the psychotherapeutic modality, which has been called the "talking treatment."

I was convinced that working with the whole family was less threatening, more logical, realistic and effective than with only the individual who was in conflict with the family, as was the prevailing practice at the time.

This revolutionary concept was only about ten years old and practiced at the time by very few in the state of Texas. After two years in my present position working with individual families, I proposed working with several families in a group. Group therapy with individuals was becoming popular, but no one in my area was working with groups of families.

I also believed a home setting was necessary. I had practiced previously in several institutional settings and had observed how distressing it was for a disturbed person to be taken from his family and home and entered into a treatment program with strangers in a strange regimented setting. I observed that the counseling techniques, a form of advice giving, were rarely successful in assisting people to change. I found that innovative communication techniques tailored to group family therapy as well as concepts and methods derived from the theatre, and the method of play therapy (employed at the time primarily by child therapists) not only accelerated learning but made it pleasurable.

I had learned the value of providing a tranquil and inviting atmosphere. It seemed one could not overestimate the value of cheerful and colorful walls, draperies, carpets and comfortable, distinctive furniture.

This kind of setting which I initiated in my positions in several institutions eliminated fear and minimized the resistance of the patient entering treatment.

It is universally accepted in our field that the first task of the therapist is to establish a trusting relationship with the patient and the first stage of the therapy must be a state of relaxation. I believed that the ambiance of a setting contributes significantly to this state. There were those at the time in the early 60's who claimed professionalism dictated reserved approaches with little or no emotion expressed. It was my opinion that these professionals in every category from nurse to physician confused lack of objectivity with personal concern.

I had found in my graduate training period, with the encouragement of an unusual psychoanalyst, that it was possible to unlock the emotional blocks and mysteries of the past without lengthy analysis if it was worthwhile to the patients and if they had the assistance from a therapist willing to explore and be creative.

I was now ready to apply the knowledge accruing from my experience to my new practice. For this I needed to buy a house.

My friend, Tom Henderson, an experienced realtor suggested a small three bedroom bungalow on the corner of Ardath Street, a neighborhood that I remembered 15 years ago had been considered very desirable. Now newer sections with more modern homes claimed that distinction. I hesitated – it would be my first year in private practice completely on my own and my first purchase of a house. But the realtor explained that the house, a repossessed property, could be bought for much under the market, $7000.00. He assured me the house was structurally sound and should be a good investment and living and working there I could deduct half of all expenses of the property. The thought of this convenience was not to be denied. Uppermost in my thinking was a chance to design a beautiful welcoming place for troubled clients.

We met at the General Hospital so Mr. Henderson could show me how convenient the location was. I was aware there could arise emergencies requiring hospitalization.

The other houses on the street were what I expected and similar to the proposed site, all built in the 40's and 50's but not yet completely emerged from the bungalow influence of the 30's.

The corner bungalow we stopped at, from its faded exterior and ragged porch railings looked indeed like one repossessed, but just for a moment. Noting the generous front porch, the two front entrances facing the street, and a yard of St. Augustine grass and Barberry shrubbery, I saw my house. The second entrance opening to what would become the waiting room cinched it.

Sherds – a Mémoire

I knew Benjamin Moore chocolate brown paint and marshmallow white trim would obliterate its graying frame and last for years. The wooden railings I would replace with cast ironwork I recalled from my family friends' Government Street home close to downtown Mobile. My mind held a reservoir of decorative Victorian ornaments I loved as an adolescent growing up in Mobile.

I signed the papers and called the carpenter recommended by Mr. Henderson. I described to him the image of the house I had in mind. He blinked and bit hard on his cigar as he listened to my color choices for walls and floors but agreed to everything. Fortunately he was a licensed electrician and plumber. Mr. Henderson emphasized he was of German descent and of the old school, exacting and particular about everything.

While the carpenter was immersed in his work I sought out second hand stores and to my delight found antiques at second hand prices. Light fixtures to me were the jewelry of the house, so I was pleased to find glass ones from the 30's in iridescent crystal and carnival glass and Tiffany type chandeliers.

Beginning with the waiting room my furniture selections included a Pennsylvania Dutch washstand, the back wall made of green tiles with yellow tulips, to serve as a desk where clients could fill out my questionnaire. Glistening golden nylon panels bought at the Dollar Store matched the color of the carpet I had chosen, undauntingly avoiding a more conservative color.

The chairs were mahogany with wooden arms magically restored to their burnished origins by furniture polish. The colors of the satin upholstery were red and bronze. There were two tall green Sheffelera plants in two foot wide creamy white pots at opposite corners. There were three small golden oak children's chairs, a Shirley Temple doll, a Buddy dolly, and a brown plush dog alongside.

The living room with the main entrance became the group room for the families. There were a beige sofa and a love seat for those choosing to sit together and a dozen arm chairs in beige and green. For the kitchen, I chose chocolate brown wallpaper and white trimmed cabinets which adjoined the living room where clients would be invited to help themselves to coffee and cookies. Some of my colleagues rolled their eyes at this practice. The first thing I was taught as a young girl about being a hostess was to make visitors feel at home by offering refreshments. I saw no reason to discontinue this courtesy in my office-home.

My collie, Daisy, joined the groups during the day but preferred to sit under the large pecan tree in the back yard at night in her self-designated role as vigilant guardian. I was at home and at work in the manner of the old physicians I had known as a child. I never had so little money, with fewer needs nor more secure feelings than in that home pursuing the job of my own design. My situation I believed was perfect. I was divorced but not alone. Friends both old and new were frequent visitors. Clients became friends as we created a new world in what I believed was an artful atmosphere. The house I had changed from an abandoned relic became for me a cottage enchanted by change.

I must admit one flaw, there was only one. The windows could not be opened. The carpenter had emphasized that they could not be repaired and should be replaced. However the cost would amount to almost as much as the cost of the house. As was typical of old houses there were many large windows. I laughed and told him the new central air conditioner he had insisted on had used up all the allocation of funds, so it would have to supply all the ventilation.

One night many months later I heard what sounded like banging coming from the outside of the back bedroom. Daisy was barking in frenzy and I heard an accompanying sound that might be coming from an animal. I suddenly recalled a night a few years before when another dog encountered a skunk in my yard which was threatening her puppies. I turned on the light outside and called Daisy inside. She would not come in, continuing to bark wildly.

After a half hour she came to the back door. Looking her over, I saw that she was unharmed. She settled down by my bedside for the rest of the night, rising occasionally to go to the window and look out.

The next morning as I was at breakfast listening to the radio I heard the announcer describe a break-in at 19002 Ardath Street. A man had entered the house through a bedroom window and raped and severely beaten a 72-year-old woman who was later taken to the hospital.

The number of my house was 19000. I realized then what the banging on my house and Daisy's barking was about. The one imperfection of the house, the windows that could not be opened, may have saved my life. Oh, yes, and thanks also to my perfect watchdog, Daisy.

Sherds

There'll be no sherds of leaves
on my pale carpet anymore
or tufts of auburn fur
or threads from trailing strings
and rugs all rumpled from a running spree
and brambles of twigs that cling
to everything
when he is gone
I think of this
when in exasperation and pain
I bend to pick them up
and set the room in order
then find one more
as company's at the door.

He does not always mind
having one of his own
and when we walk he has a look which says
no this way this way,
but this is natural for an Alpha dog
and well I've been a Beta all my life

So now when I observe
these multi assaults on my decorum
I think – he's here – at least for now
and smile
He has not gone he's here!
Still mine awhile.

Perspectives

A poet does not view a cloud
custodian of rain
but architect of castles
a pirate ship a train

And in the whine of winter winds
a wolverine at bay
a puppy's whimper mother's moan
a call from one away

And antique lover is the same
a poet through and through
at fashioning a parlor lamp
from burnished wornout shoe

And hanging on my bathroom wall
a kitchen tool bright-sprayed
to hold an antique towel
there for my guests arrayed

Cinderella is a cookie jar
a bottle's a Christmas tree
for use on an occasion
but mainly there for me

A green ash tray derelict
becomes a serving bowl
and every kind of quaintness
loved because it's old

To the poetic antique lover
old's revered preserved and free,
as poetry is living art
antiques tout history

Around a captivating thought
poet muses at her desk
annihilates the mundane word

to seize the picturesque

Cherishing the secret thrill
(even if never heard)
 the poet tells her story
with a solitary word

The poet's nourished as she writes
reborn as she re-reads
and antiques lover imbibes the soul
of relics she only sees

Chapter 13 – Commentaries

South Carolina – Dear Connection

Ann Wolfe Jacobson

The picture of Camden, South Carolina in the 1920's and 1930's hangs in my mind like an old fashioned picture post card. It was more than my good fortune to have spent most of my childhood summers and several Christmas vacations there. My father was born and raised there and determined that his daughter should experience some of her growing up in the environment he loved and was proud of.

My trips to Camden by myself on the Crescent Limited train were always exciting. Looking through the wide windows at night from the lower berth and eating in the dining car while enjoying the scenery could never be rivaled by dining before the television.

When my father drove me to Camden the first thing he would do would be to take me to the revered locations of this town which were rich in Revolutionary War history. We would stand for a long time before the statues, read the legends on the monuments, and walk slowly through the old cemeteries. His grandfather, an immigrant from Prussia in 1840 served in the Civil War. He pointed out the inn where Lafayette had visited and the bank where in past years my Great Uncle Dave was president.

The four great aunts in their late fifties and the two aunts in their forties, whose houses together occupied a square block, and the six cousins, some my own age welcomed me as one of the children.

They encouraged me to explore the small quaint downtown district, which I did walking the few blocks from Great Aunt Minnie's house where I always stayed on my visits. Several of the family members were merchants and either ran or owned some of the department and grocery stores. A surprise gift accompanied every visit to the stores: a handkerchief, a straw hat, some hair ribbons, and on one occasion a black wool coat circa 1910 from Uncle Isadore's tiny, dark cavern-like store, with garments and iron tools hung on nails from the wall. Aunt Minnie was "aghast" at her brother-in-law's "rediculous" present to her twelve year old niece who nevertheless was thrilled with her unique coat which covered her shoe-tops.

Every female relative, including my second cousin Sarah, seemed to outdo the others with a party for me. Even I knew this was excess and too much for a child. There were also some family friends who called themselves "aunt." They lived in much smaller houses, and although their tables were not so fancy or full, they extended the same gracious welcome to me. One of them "Aunt" Ramona with her long dark hair and eyes and inviting smile looked like a Spanish character of the movies. Her attentions were sincere and she always told how much she enjoyed my visits. I learned from her and all I met in Camden how real hospitality had nothing to do with how much or how little one owned. I have been grateful for the memory of these years when harsh times and persons changed my life.

Better than the parties were the everyday mealtimes. All of the aunts set linens, china, crystal, and silverware, and often flowers from their gardens on large oval tables with not three or four vegetable dishes as was my mother's habit, but twice that number. Mother was shocked when she heard of such "over-indulgence" especially in the depression times. I told her there were always extra guests at mealtimes.

Breakfast was a grand event. Nothing gives a better picture of the life and time I experienced in Camden than breakfast at Great Aunt Minnie's. One learned from the conversation of this diminutive matriarch that she was a leader in the community as well as in her family. Her husband, Uncle Mannes, presided at the head of the table while Aunt Minnie sat at the other end close to the kitchen with easy access for orders to the cook. To the left of Uncle Mannes sat Uncle Joe, his brother, and wife Aunt Hattie who occupied an apartment in the twenty-two room house. Aunt Hattie, a silver haired lady in her 50's was elegant even at breakfast with her fashionable upswept hair and garments which hinted at distant markets. She said little, but her actions and manners commanded attention.

Uncle Joe, a burly jovial man about the same age as his wife, commented on every issue brought up in the very spirited discussions. He maintained a boat on a nearby island off the coast of South Carolina, and I always fantasized him as a sea captain. The most talkative at the table were both men as they discussed business and politics.

Next to Aunt Minnie on the other side of the table sat Aunt Caroline. "Aunt Carrie," as she was called, would invite me to come upstairs to her apartment after breakfast and see her collections of jewelry, scarves, and feathers. She favored blue, as she said, "They compliment my China blue eyes." She evoked Aunt Minnie's impatience daily as they waited for Uncle Mannes to return from their farm bringing fruits and cheeses, adding to the sausage, bacon, eggs, and biscuits on the sideboard. "I hope he returns with my clabber," she would repeat every day, "that's all I want for breakfast." Aunt Minnie's response was always the same, "With all this food and you only want clabber! You'll waste away, Sister."

There were usually three or more cousins present. Debbie, my age, inched her way to sit on Uncle Mannes's lap until she saw Aunt Minnie's stern, staring eyes. Carolyn from my mother's side of the family was a constant companion. We remained good friends after we were grown. David, a silver-blond, thin young man offered himself as escort to every event during the summer. The other three older cousins, Sarah, the school teacher, Julian and Simon, the young businessmen who worked in their father's store dropped in occasionally. There was room for all at this family table. Breakfast at the Baruch household became the dining model for me. One of the most lasting impressions of those Camden years was my decision to view meals not as routine necessity, but to regard them as celebration of food for family and friends.

Visits to Camden in the ensuing years provided some perspective for observing changes brought about by aging, the attendant weakening and passing of family members. I observed the Aunts' reddish-blond hair become gray, and the great aunts' arthritic fingers, and I guessed at my legacy.

But I did not foresee the end of this congenial and lovely community. Many years later my companion Bill and I made a visit to Camden so that he might see some of the beautiful sights of my youth. We drove down the familiar street with the antebellum and Victorian mansions and arrived at the spot to find only a large parking lot adjoining a large church. And then I recalled Aunt Minnie saying she would leave her property to the

Methodist Church next door, because they were such good neighbors and allowed her congregation to hold services there on Friday nights.

After the shock of seeing the empty parking lot instead of the anticipated view, I burst into tears. Then I was ready to drive home, but we made a quick tour of the town. Everything was changed except the cemeteries – they were remarkably well kept and beautiful.

On the way home I became absorbed with the thought of what was left for me to carry away from the scenes. The mental picture of the mansions and quaint downtown business section was undimmed; as well as the many good times and gifts from those generous family members, and oddly enduringly the breakfast gathering at Aunt Minnie's board. This more than all the rest remains the metaphor for rewarding good times, entertaining company, and family solidarity.

Riding the Bus

Riding the bus for me was never merely a means of transportation to a destination, rather a favorite recreation sure to produce excitement capped with a surprise.

I think this originated in the streetcar rides as a child when my Grandfather would take my two younger brothers and me every Thursday to the Grand Theatre in Atlanta. The appointed day was Thursday, because this was when Linda our beloved nurse, as we called our black caretakers in those days, took her day off duty.

We looked forward all week to the long walk from our house on Linwood Avenue to the streetcar stop on Ponce de Leon Avenue and the long way around to downtown Atlanta which offered Granddaddy the opportunity to point out and describe the Civil War monuments and old office buildings and factories on the way. Granddaddy exploited his storyteller talents as he chose different examples on each trip. He made sure we remembered the historical dates, purposes, and the pioneer businessmen who created them. His favorite was the Levi Strauss pants and overall factory where he had worked as a young man, and his encounters with the man himself on his occasional visits from California. Granddaddy would enact for us the shouting matches he would have with Mr. Strauss on the proper way to cut men's pants.

In the 50s and 60s riding the bus became the popular mode of transportation and the promise of the ride had not diminished. The Trailways and the Greyhound Buses were not uncomfortable though certainly not luxurious. One could push the seat back and rest and footrests were provided. I remember the upholstery as being grey and fuzzy and not made for looks.

Riding the bus continued to be an adventure. Now instead of only riding past inviting sites, I could take advantage of the frequent local stops and explore the villages for twenty minutes or so when the bus driver always went inside for a cup of coffee. The mom and pop stores attached to the bus stop were intriguing. It was fun exploring homespun garments and oddities for sale, scarves and sunbonnets as well as cookies and candies. Best of all was making new friends on the road trip.

Sherds – a Mémoire

It is ironic that my most memorable bus trip was both a surprise and a disappointment. Oddly now I cannot remember whether it was in Texas or on my way to Alabama, but it was in the 50s I'm sure of that.

After boarding the bus and handing the driver my ticket I looked around the very crowded scene for a seat. About three fourths back of the bus was a vacant seat next to an attractive young black woman. She was neatly dressed in a blue tailored suit and hat, wearing hose and pumps. The only other seat was further up toward the front next to one occupied by a white man. Seeing his dirty face and unkempt appearance, I chose to sit down by the woman.

The driver started away, then looking in the rear view mirror to see if all the passengers were settled in their seats, drove a few yards to the side of the road and stopped, opening the door. He walked back to my seat and standing over me, he ordered sternly,

"Miss, you'll have to move up and take a seat by that man."

"I prefer to stay here," I told the driver.

"I say you'll have to move," he was firm and glowering above me.

I didn't reply or move.

After a moment the woman stood up and moved quietly to the last single row across the end of the bus where half a dozen black people were seated. They all moved aside to make room for her to squeeze in. I continued to stay where I was, while the driver continued to stand over me, his jaw muscles twitching. I was sure he would ask me to leave the bus. He opened his mouth to say something.

"Miss," he faltered.

I looked him in the eye and my words came out between clenched teeth,

"Yes?" I suspect it sounded like a hiss. He waited a moment more then slowly returned to his seat, closed the door and drove off.

I know now I must have been frightened and concerned for my safety on the rest of the trip, as the driver's expression transferred to the faces of the passengers, with their accompanying mumbling, like low growls, which I was sure were not in my favor.

The remainder of the trip was without incident, and I departed at my stop with a look back to the woman in the rear of the bus. The friendly looks on the faces of the others beside her made me feel good.

The situation did not require nerve or courage on my part. Being in the midst of this kind of threatening situation where I chose to challenge the status quo had occurred several times before. I used to say this was my frequent "briar patch."

My role models had prepared and sustained me: my Mother who taught me to treat every person rich or poor, black or white, educated or not with respect while purporting myself in a dignified manner; my Father, who in the Depression refused to pay his servants the wage condoned by his neighbors because he believed the black person was owed a living wage as much as a white person; and finally Linda, the young and dignified gentle servant, who was my caretaker as well as my teacher and companion throughout my childhood and who modeled serenity in every situation.

"Linda, I will name my little girl after you," I had promised. Unfortunately I had no children. My little brother was present and heard me. His daughter's name is Linda.

They Say I Mustn't read Little Black Sambo Now

They say I mustn't read Little Black Sambo now
it's not "correct" it's not respectful now
that's odd because that's how I learned respect,
Respect you say and how could that be? How?

Look what Black Mumbo did: she cut and sewed
and by her efforts clothed her son in beauty
Black Jumbo always worked so had the money
to buy those purple shoes and green umbrella

(could I forget those crimson soles and linings!)

And how did Little Black Sambo show respect?
Right off he greeted every tiger properly
and said, "Please, Mr. Tiger" to every one of them.

And right away you see how enterprising
our Sambo was and very helpful too
to those three tigers who didn't know how to dress.

I also learned that claiming to be grander
than someone else can lead to heated anger
then argument and finally to fighting
and in the end goals, friends and self are lost.

I learned how fighting- - the tigers did you know - -
was not near smart as a negotiation
and when our Sambo sought to claim his clothes
he had the courtesy before he did so
to ask the tigers if they wanted them.

Black Jumbo came and saw an opportunity
and figured how to bring a harvest home,
Black Mumbo was respectful not to question
but used the butter in a mess of pancakes.

And there I learned of stories' happy endings

and that taught me how my own life could be
if I'm respectful and also enterprising.

My Chosen Subject

Suddenly everyone is writing about Abraham Lincoln these days, authors, journalists, in newspapers, magazines, writers of every rank and party, cataloguing his traits, his achievements, his language. I wrote about Lincoln too, not as scholarly or eloquently, but I was only 10 years old. I was in the 5th grade in history class in Atlanta, September 1928.

Calvin Coolidge was president, and my parents, both interested in teaching us the importance of history, discussed the relative merits of the presidents, past and recent, ardently and frequently.

So I came confidently to the assignment of my history teacher to deliver a speech on our favorite president. It was not as flowery as my previous speech on Balboa discovering the Pacific Ocean or delivered as breathlessly, but I noted at the time my teacher spent more time on Balboa than on my subject, Abraham Lincoln. I covered the essentials, dealing with his humble birth and upbringing in a log cabin.

The houses I was brought up in were imprinted on my persona and influenced my view of the world: my Grandfather's Victorian house on Washington Street; the smaller Bungalow on Greenwood Avenue; and the finest of them all, the present red brick and white trimmed home surrounded by a variety of fruit trees and spruce and juniper evergreens. So I was impressed that President Lincoln was born in a small log cabin and studied by firelight.

I had begun to read poetry at home before the first grade, such writers as Wordsworth and Tennyson. Poetry to me was not merely pretty thoughts written prettily. I had lain on my sick bed for months at that age and looked out each day on a fence with sweetheart roses and banks of yellow daffodils. I too felt I "wandered lonely as a cloud" and drew strength from the sight of daffodils, and Wordsworth's view of them became part of my own identity.

I felt the same about Lincoln's words as I read them. I could imagine reading my own books by the firelight of our living room fireplace.

I began the speech,
"My favorite President is Abraham Lincoln. He was born poor, lived in a log cabin and lay on a bare, hard floor as he studied his lessons by firelight." I considered this condition must have been the most important thing in his life, because wouldn't a person raised with an appreciation of everything available to him from books motivate him to want education for his

countrymen? No wonder his words were eloquent as they embodied earthy elements and enduring high values of all the great ones he studied.

I recall now only the first sentence but felt I had given a good speech. In the past I had received good grades in this class. I looked to the teacher assured of the approval certain to follow. She looked at me sideways out of those dark eyes of hers, the perfect match to her cold black straight hair drawn severely into a bun at the back. Her voice was cold and thin, "It looks like you could have chosen a better President."

Here was the main lesson of the day: all teachers would be guided by their valued beliefs and these would determine the course of their teaching. I would observe this in myself when I became a teacher, and understand some years afterward my professors' judgments of me, as their personal opinions adorned their courses like garlands.

The Thief

Today the newspaper ran a classic tale, a homeless old man was arrested for stealing a small box of donuts. His defense: he was hungry. He was arrested as a thief.

I was a thief once too, but I was never caught. I was 8 years old. I was on my way home from school when a group of girls asked me to join them. I did not know them well, though Mary Ann who seemed to be the leader of the group had visited in my house on Linwood Avenue in Atlanta. Mary Ann said they were going north on Ponce de Leon Avenue to the drug store.

It was a small drug store I had never been in before. The cosmetic counter with bath powder and perfume attracted my attention. I reached in my pocket for the coin my Father had given me that morning. The rest of the girls formed a semicircle in front of the candy counter. Realizing my dime was useless at the cosmetic counter I joined the others. Mary Ann whispered, "Let's steal a candy bar."

I was startled. No thoughts came to my head. After a moment I could not say no and maybe cause an argument and get others in trouble. My hand went to a 5 cent Baby Ruth candy bar, slipped it into my pocket and I walked slowly to the sidewalk as if in a trance.

The others ran down the street, but I stopped in front of the store. I couldn't move. Slowly I became aware that I had stolen something. My head felt hot as the Sunday School lesson about the Commandments surfaced. It prompted a question. I asked myself, "Why did I do that? I had a dime in my hand." The answer was immediate, "Because someone else said to do it, someone I called a friend."

That was the first time I had ever asked myself about my motivation in a situation.

And as it happens when I ask myself a question I receive an answer in full, "because a friend issued an order and I obeyed, not wanting to oppose what the majority clearly wanted to do. Not wanting to be different. Not wanting to stand alone."

The last part summoned up my Mother's favorite admonition. "Don't be a sheep."

My body ached with guilt, but I was too afraid to go back inside and confess the deed to the manager. Then I felt doubly guilty. I had committed a crime and was not brave enough to do anything to correct it.

I also could not face telling my parents, who of course would ask many questions and punish me in their usual way by denying me something I had asked for. It was not the punishment that frightened me, it was the fear of the shame I would feel in their presence. Punishment from them would be unnecessary, this 8-year-old judge had meted out the judgment and the sentence. I laid the candy bar on the brick ledge of the store window. It was not an act of penance, the candy bar was an awful thing I must put away from me.

However, this act did not resolve my punishing quilt. I must think about it and worry and try to figure out why I was unable to stop myself doing something I knew was wrong.

I learned several lessons from the incident. The first was easy. I would never steal again. I could not be sure that I would not temporarily be stalled again when others chose a forbidden action. But I would not join the action just to be "one of the crowd." I would stop and think. I would not be afraid to be different.

I learned what I consider to be the key to the development of self-awareness; to ask oneself the motivations in a situation of conflict and decision-making. Which is one of the reasons I was able to become a psychotherapist. Because of this particular experience I was able to be helpful to children and adults who had developed obsessions as a result of a similar transgression when very young but had never developed the tools for resolution.

The One That Got Away

I have a thousand memories
with treasured things to match
but even my best friends will say
my home's a booby hatch

I have a gown for any event
to make me feel charismal
but friends who dare to steal a peak
say my closets are abysmal.

The sixteen mirrors in my house
defy the term simplistic
but what else can a person do
who's simply narcissistic?

I walk my dog in full attire
or holiday design
and never fear for safety as
folks waving drive close by

My dog's large antique basket
is bottomless with choice
but walking through my bedroom
beware the obstacle course

But with all this abundance
I'm sorry, friends to say
I'll always grieve a little
for the one that got away

For on that fateful day I thought

a gain essential then
for alas I sold my treasure
for a sum much less than ten

And oh it was a real antique
unique so I was told
I knew it when I bought it
I knew it when I sold

And you may wonder how it is
that I'll grieve evermore
for the matchsafe with the logo
"Love and Let Live Grocery Store"

A House Speaks

I am most proud, I guess, of my floors, golden oak, cedar red and walnut brown. Yes, all of these I have. I'm pleased with the small, octagon white tiles in the bathrooms. I am a very old house you know, and it is no little thing to have more than one bathroom. It's a feat of endurance when the tiles look good after 75 years. You can tell to look at me I have been cared for.

The trees in the grove nearby are the real owners of the floors. The tile came from out west, the product of artisans.

So you must surely know how I felt when the winds drove the rain roughshod over my floors. The colors disappeared in the mold and mildew that invaded them. The rain and the wind spared the walls, which were left intact. The iridescent chandeliers shone unscathed.

I was always made happy by color; my walls made me feel strong, and my chandeliers tickled my fantasy.

Now I'm told the floors must go, must be completely replaced. Replaced? Something else taking their place? Not likely.

Perhaps you think I should feel relieved. Perhaps you think they can be restored by the trees still standing in the grove. How could they be the same?

Perhaps I should be grateful. But I am too sad to be generous.

It is said that floors are the structural and decorative foundation of every room. But to me they are my heart.

Canine Selectivity

My dog, an able communicator
uses his eyes and voice
to make his relatively few needs known
he stares the stare of the Sheepdog and barks
his varied barks discriminately
when he decides it's time to eat or drink or walk
or survey his yard.

Sometimes he cries,
he doesn't cry when his loving
veterinarian sticks a needle in his vein
he doesn't cry when I sweep the floor,
or vacuum or cook or dress
or any kind of work
except writing.

Then he cries.

Chapter 14 – Letters To The Editor

August 1966

August 1, 1966, is a specific date I had forgotten, but not the day, nor the tragedies that occurred, nor the small part I played in that horrific event.

I was walking at the time from the central office of the Department of Mental Health Mental Retardation in Austin, Texas and heading to the library of the University of Texas and the Tower to research material for a project on mental illness. A psychiatric social worker, I was employed by the department. I stopped for a moment on the Drag a couple of blocks up from the walkway in front of the bookstore to look at a table in the window of a small antique shop. As I went inside someone shouted, "They're shooting people on the campus!" It was the radio, then suddenly shouts came from everywhere.

After a few minutes listening to reports, I left and went back the way I came to the department office. Back there everyone stopped to listen to the broadcasts until closing time.

The next morning, as I prepared to leave for work, I saw several small boys from the neighborhood sitting on a bench in my backyard. They appeared to be waiting for something. They had often come to visit, calling out, "Can Daisy come out and play?" Daisy was my collie. This morning, however, they were just sitting, strangely silent, their eyes searching mine and waiting for me to speak.

I put down my notebook and purse and sat with them. I knew they had something serious on their minds. Then I noticed one of the boys was handling a length of braided plastic material, like a key chain. It was orange and white. I asked the boy to tell me about it. Then he blurted out, "I'm making a Tower!" At that, all the others started talking at once, asking about the shootings, saying their parents "wanted the lady from the hospital to tell them about it and why it had happened." We talked a long time until they had no more questions or comments and felt ready to go home. I was late to work that day.

In a few days, I returned to my research at the library. I remember feeling phobic as I made myself go back. Looking up at the Tower, I remember telling myself I had to face my fears and continue on. I had learned about such things in my work.

I was not as close to the tragedies as the author of the Alcalde story in the alumni magazine, but like her and undoubtedly countless others, the memories of those 40-year-old campus scenes are still vivid. And I've never forgotten the lessons of that spontaneous children's conference or the boy's words, "I'm making a Tower."

Jule Jacobson Moon
BA '40, MA '41, MSSW '63
Fairhope, Ala.

Displaced Thinking Can Lead to Violence

The Oct. 4 article on the Nickel Mines School tragedy ("Experts struggle to understand school shooting") revived some 30-year-old memories, particularly the quote, "The murder of the girls is hard to understand from a psychological viewpoint."

In my former practice of psychotherapy, with some dangerous and self-destructive individuals, my goal was to understand and redirect the patients' displaced thinking.

These patients discussed violent fantasies and dreams involving hurt experienced years before. They described wishes and intentions to bring violent harm to others. In efforts to rid themselves of anguish and eliminate what they believed to be the sources of their problems, they would express these needs by harming others who symbolized the original offenders.

Not having learned to resolve issues in a satisfying and constructive way, they resorted to infantile, aggressive retaliation for perceived injury. Patients who were unable to benefit from medical treatment were referred to me for psychotherapy.

A bizarre example was the wife of a young firefighter, referred by an orthopedist because she struck her husband across the kneecap with a hammer when he returned home from a fire to which he had been called. The blow was intended to convey to him the pain she had "felt from his neglect."

She had refused to talk to him about her action. The baffled husband and the still-angry wife consented to talk with me about the incident.

When asked what she was thinking when she struck the blow, she said she was angry because her husband had left the house in a hurry and had failed to kiss her goodbye, which she interpreted to mean he did not love her any more, and she wanted him to feel her hurt. She felt justified in her reaction.

The irrationality of this act meant nothing to her, only her hurt and the need for him to feel it. The husband now said he understood her and they promised to talk to each other about their feelings when problems arose in the future. He realized they never talked. She must learn to talk instead of hit.

Another example of displaced violent behavior concerns a continually angry, talented young sculptor who obsessively fantasized about blowing up his parents' home. His description of his dreams revealed a history of feeling ridiculed and not being appreciated at home, school and at work.

Over a period of months in individual group therapy, he gradually came to value himself, regardless of others' opinions. Finally, I referred him to a psychiatrist, a likely positive male figure. I told the patient that if he should ever feel the need to express his hostility in a destructive way, he should call me at any hour before he reacted.

Some months later, he phoned me at work to say that in a few minutes there would be a ceremony at his university in which the president would make a presentation of his sculpture to honor his body of work.

He said he had decided to demolish the sculpture with a sledge hammer. He intended to make a statement by this act so they would know how he felt about having been rejected over the years as a student.

I asked him if there was a way he could get his point over, while not being hostile and self-destructive, and did he not think that in fact the head of the university making the presentation was indeed acknowledging him as an outstanding artist?

I recall he liked the phrase "acknowledging him as an outstanding artist." He then made the decision to accept the public honor without retaliating. In the end, his need for acceptance was greater than his urge to destroy.

JULE MOON
Fairhope

The Sniper

A library search propelled me to the Tower,
important documents for my assignment
the hour though late I strolled the street day-dreaming
the familiar friendly street changed little these twenty years
being a college town

A table through a window was arresting
a picnic table cedar-red hand-hewn
and old the very thing to grace my country yard
and please my guests come Saturday for supper

The antiques dealer smiled and bade me enter
happy to see his wares appreciated
the price twenty dollars and delivery agreeable
our arrangement swift I noticed the old radio still working

and then the interruption an announcer shouting
"Someone is shooting people from the Tower!"
disbelief and horror as we listened
the messenger crying out the numbers stricken

And then my thought - natural human reaction -
but for my antiques lust and meandering
I'd be among them

And now today still decades from that hour
I ask to what I owe my lucking sparing?
At the very least a habit of day-dreaming
and interrupting goals for a diversion

Chapter 15 – The Pageant

L-R: Jule Marion Jacobson Moon, Delores Palmer-Bert, Hilda Vickers,
Charlotte Below, Helen Wright, Rosemary Harris in the
Mrs. Senior Baldwin County Pageant of 2005.

It was June, the birthday month of my 86th year. I was in a self-congratulatory mood, indulging in a mental inventory of the state of my health.

I had a new set of eyes that could see more than 8 feet away without glasses for the first time in my life, thanks to implants from cataract surgery; a partial knee replacement – a hunk of metal and plastic for cartilage long gone in my right knee; I had maintained 10 pounds of weight loss for four years due to my own common sense observation and diagnosis and method of subtracting the fattening culprits from my diet; I was still singing soprano in two choral groups and singing and playing the drum in a folk singing band.

My hair was thinner and grey under my regular 8 weeks application of blond toner. I had shrunk 1½ inches, and I had quit looking for wrinkles, as they were apparent without a second glance. All in all I mused, I was content with my restoration, when the phone rang and interrupted my reverie.

A cultured, musical voice introduced itself: My name is Nancy, and I represent the Mrs. Senior Baldwin County Pageant of 2005, those ladies who have attained the age of elegance, sixty. You have been recommended to qualify as a contestant. I had to ask a second time, "Who is this?"

Repeating the first message she added, "A friend of yours who was also asked to compete but who is too young, she's 58, recommended you."

I laughed loudly and rudely asked again, "Who is this?" I was trying to figure out which one of my jokester friends was pulling my new leg.

"No, no," she said, telling her name again, and this time her place of residence, and repeated her message.

Calming down a bit and chancing that she was on the up and up I asked, "Do you know how old I am?" She did. "Am I the oldest one to enter?"

"Yes, again."

I paused.

She went on gaily, "The oldest one ever."

That settled it! I was the oldest, at least some questionable distinction. 'What do I have to do?"

"Sing," she said, "and wear a gorgeous gown with lots of glitz, dance in a chorus line, be interviewed by 3 expert pageant judges who will ask you anything about your life, present a synopsis of your life accomplishments for the newspaper, one page only, which will also be read to the audience by the Mistress of Ceremonies as you promenade on the stage in your dress, and tell your philosophy of life in 30 seconds."

So, *OK*, I thought, I have a gown and it won't cost me anything.

The first meeting was orientation and a critique of our gowns by the Directors. Ten tables were spread out against the walls of a large room, the contestants at attention beside them while the Directors came by to judge each gown and accessories. It was very quiet; it was apparent the choice of the gown was important.

Mine was an all over black lace floor-length gown with embroidered flowers at the waist, brought to me from Mexico 33 years ago as a gift from an admirer. It was a collectible. I had even worn it to the Annual Grand Summer Ball, at the Grand Hotel.

Sherds – a Mémoire

The Directors conferred aloud, frowned, and shook their heads in unison, "It won't do."

I said, "It looks better on."

They said, "Not enough glitz. You'll look like Cinderella before the ball."

So there it was. I'd have to spend big bucks after all and, worst of all, go to Mobile and try on dresses all day.

I set out with diminished confidence for the shopping trip. But passing the Goodwill Store I thought, *Maybe with a little bit of luck....*

I went straight to the evening gown rack with about five gowns. I saw it right away, a purple silk vision with 500,000 bugle beads (the Directors had already prepared me, they are the glitziest) and lots of sequins. It fit. I would be Cinderella *at* the ball. Cost $32.00.

The Directors loved it. "Where did you get it? How much did it cost?"

To tell or not to tell? I told. They loved it: Goodwill, cost and all.

Guess who won the "Best Dressed Trophy?"

The afternoon of the pageant event arrived. The stage show was spectacular, a hit. The audience was packed, including many dignitaries, the mayor, and the National Guard.

I held my own with the contestants, I sang OK, but my microphone went out in the first few bars, and I changed three words in the philosophy of life, a blunder which cost me 12 points in the counting of credits. My synopsis of accomplishments included discovering a dinosaur track, but another contestant was a pilot and another was the president of several companies. Anyway, I was an also ran, not placing 1,2, or 3, for Queen.

It was a thrill to see the large contingent of friends from the neighborhood, church, and some of my clubs in the audience who came to support me. I could hear them cheering my performance. A gentleman whom I had never met came up to me, took both my hands in his and whispered, "You should have won." Even if he said it to the others I appreciated it.

Next day at church a stranger came up to me and presented me with a bouquet of 6 dozen roses and 6 dozen spring flowers. A woman called that day, "You don't know me," she said, "but although I'm leaving in a few minutes to return home to North Carolina, I want to tell you how much you have inspired me to make a change in my own life and start performing again. I've been idle too long."

Actually I think all of us in the pageant were hoping to be role models for the older women who need a little push to be more active in their chosen vocations.

T[...] came from a good friend (Dr. Helen Conwell) whom I'[...] we were girls, "We wuz robbed." That was worth a rhines[...]

Self Portrait

On greeting my image in the mirror on my 87th birthday

On greeting my image in the mirror on my 87th birthday

My crinkly wrinkles above my lips
are epitaphs for men I've kissed
my two deep grooves between my eyes
are signatures of sunny skies

The crows' feet perched beneath my brow
are all my humor could endow
my dimples once like Shirley Temple's
are now just wrinkles plain and simple

The semicircles round my cheeks
are brave derivatives from leaps
to please the world by words and deeds
and smiles to cover unmet needs

But he who saw me young inside
left me with no need to hide
and so I'll keep this blemished skin
reminding me of all I've been

Diagnosis

When I was young
I heard old folks say
see that old woman walking walking
talking talking to herself
she's fey.

It's funny now I see
poets sitting sitting
writing writing to themselves
are they?

Some say the fey ones
are lonely the reason
they do what they do
are poets lonely too?

Ode to a Purse

Oh give me a purse
not one that's perverse
where the keys and sunglasses play
hide and go seek
with nary a peek
from my eyes as they tunnel away,

where the lipstick and comb
continually roam
'neath the Kleenex, compact, and pomade,
where there's always more room
for cell phone and perfume,
bobby pins, emery board, and hairspray.

I long for the days
when a bag was a purse,
not a tote, not a satchel, not a sack,
my bangled arm free
attached just to me,
not harnessed as horse to a pack.

Autumn Reverie

Some memories have no words
only the faint sound and scent and sensing
like the one that returns every autumn
when the first cold wind
arouses the feeling I had
in my first grownup coat.

I can smell the new fabric now
as its enveloping strength and coziness
surround and protect against the cold intruder
and bring with it a familiar feeling –
and the feeling is wonder.

Body Images

You busted my budget
my fine furry guy
from vet's shots and treatments
you caused me to buy

you made me go walking
when my knees would elect
to relax on the sofa
while I muse and reflect

on the fun I could have
with the hundreds you cost
and those sweet carefree years
when I was the boss

and what can I say
when my body screams "no!"
but you and your eyes
only stare and flash "go!"

I will have to admit
you're worth all the pain
and hundreds and hundreds
all over again

but for you I would lounge
on the sofa and dream
while my body becomes
mashed potatoes and cream

The Accidental Packrat

I'm categorically opposed to hoarding
lest I'm overcome by greed
I absolutely never buy
a want instead of need

and yet a two for 1 sale holds me
hopelessly in thrall
a bargain's only saving
I tell myself—that's all.

When I change a certain item's brand
I keep the old one for the day
when the new one's discontinued
so I never throw away.

After the plumber's fixed the sink
I excavate beneath
and find three thousand que tips
I'm obligated to bequeath

Alas my clutter shows what I
deny I ever made -
those purchases stockpiled!
I'm sure some trick on me was played!

Unfortunately my memory

is accessory to the fact
that items accrue as if I'd planned
to be a stealth packrat.

And if you're the type to pile things
on that large but hidden shelf
you're in danger of becoming
and accidental packrat like myself.

Chapter 16 – Laddie's Ivan Adventure

It was 2:30 in the afternoon when the phone rang. I'm sure of the time, because that's when Mama calls me in from the yard and we observe nap time. I'm very good with time, because I know when its supper time and walk time, and it's my job to wake her up every morning before the alarm clock rings.

This day when I came in I saw water bottles and flashlights everywhere, and I heard her voice – very loud to the phone – like it sounds when I walk too near a car – and I heard her say,

"I'm staying right here! I will not leave my dog, Laddie, and go to a shelter. I don't care if the police do come and order me to leave!"

I'm very good with words too. I know that word "shelter" all too well, only I didn't know people had to go to them. Anyway she said she would not go to one, "Ivan or no Ivan!"

Then she put on her boots, which usually means we're going for a walk in the rain. But then she began gathering up the flashlights and water bottles, our toothbrushes – Mama is very insistent on brushing our teeth – my bed, blankets, boxes of dog and people food, and a large cooler of sandwiches.

Mama put these in the car and said, "We're going on a trip after we pick up Mary Ann." She's our neighbor. Mama told me, "We're the only ones still here on our block, all the others left yesterday, some staying with friends in Mobile, some headed north."

We all three sat in the front seat, mine is higher in the middle.

Mary Ann said, "Laddie, we're heading for Montgomery and we're not waiting around for Ivan!"

I supposed he was going there on his own, and we'd meet him later.

Off we went joining a long line of cars, stopping every few yards. Usually when Mama stops too long I bark to remind her to move on. There was something very different about this trip. It was eerie, lights stringing far into the distance. Mama was concentrating hard on her driving and Mary Ann was nervous, so even though it's my responsibility as a herding dog to bark, I thought it best to be quiet the whole trip. They said I was a "good dog."

After several hours we turned into a rest stop. There were many parked cars and a long line of people waiting to get into a small square building. Mama read a sign.

"Pet area."

We walked around a bit. I enjoyed the nice grass and trees. Meanwhile Mary Ann stood in line with the other people who were waiting their turn for the people's bathroom. Several of them called out to us,

"There's no tissue or paper towels in there."

Mama, an experienced traveler, had packed many rolls of each in the back seat. We passed them out to the others. They were very grateful. It was good to stop.

We drove a long time until we finally came to a very big house, they called it a motel. That was a new word. Mama said,

"We do not have a reservation."

Another new word. My breed, I'm told, is good at understanding words, and also that I have a big vocabulary. Mama read a big sign,

"NO VACANCIES."

Going inside she asked the manager if we could park close to the front door for the night. It was 2 A.M. and very dark. The manager was friendly, inviting us into the lobby and insisting that we sleep on the sofas. My bed was put on the floor, of course, which is where I sleep at home.

A few minutes later two ladies came in with 4 big dogs.

The manager said, "They have reservations."

So "they" went upstairs. Mama looked at me with wide eyes and lowered her voice in that way which means I must be on my best behavior. My instincts told me that this was very important now. Soon the lobby was full of people. They were talking about "Ivan" too, but still no "Ivan."

The next afternoon we were finally given a room. Afterwards we went walking in the rain, which is one of my favorite things, especially when there are puddles. Mama put my raincoat on me, that told me it was raining hard. I like to wear my raincoat, and people always comment and say I look handsome. Also it doubles as a costume when we walk in the Mardi Gras parade.

Next day after breakfast we heard there were some people who had no food, so we shared ours with them. They said they had to leave in a hurry and were unable to find food before they left on account of Ivan. I supposed he took it all.

For two nights after that we were in darkness, as the electricity went out, but the flashlights helped. Actually I didn't mind the dark.

After three days it was time to go home. We stopped at the desk to say goodbye to the manager and thank him for his hospitality. He said there was no charge for the dogs "under the circumstances." I guess he liked dogs. He said,

"We had a motel full."

Going back was a much better trip. We drove faster, Mary Ann was more relaxed, and Mama kept saying I "wasn't afraid of anything." I have heard some dogs are afraid of thunder and hide under the bed. Mama told me when I was little that thunder is just a loud noise and could not hurt us. Lightning, on the other hand, is a different story and nothing to fool around with. We never walk in the rain if there is lightning.

Before on the way north through Evergreen a policeman had stopped us and offered to take us to the shelter there. We thanked him but moved on. On the way back we were stopped again and told that the roof of the shelter had caved in. I guess that's why Mama didn't want to go to a shelter. I had my own reasons.

Well, we're home in Fairhope now, back to routine everyday living. I finally figured out what Ivan was. It wasn't a person after all. It was a really, really, long, slow ride to Montgomery, lots of wind and rain, three days and nights in a motel, and every meal a picnic!

Chapter 17 – Bill

I met William at the national conference for social workers in San Antonia, Texas. That was 1977, exactly 18 years after my divorce from James. He approached directly and introduced himself and escorted me to a workshop table.

I had been immersed in a heavy workload of clients in day and night family therapy group sessions, and I was relieved to be able to get away for a weekend of workshops. I expected that social activities would be included, but I did not expect a special encounter with anyone, let alone this tall blue-eyed brown-haired man who looked like a magazine model in his shirt and sport coat.

James could manage to be polite on introduction, Bill, as he liked to be called, was engaging. It was apparent here was a man who expressed his feelings in his behavior, not like a "stick" – that's what we used to call stodgy boys, when as young girls we gossiped about the boys in school.

I liked Bill immediately. He said he was an administrator in the Veteran's Administration hospital. He had been in World War II, stationed in Okinawa. He said no more about his experiences there, nor did he ever. He was now retired and if ever a person didn't fit the retiring type, it was he.

During the long coffee break we talked about our work. He had held many jobs in his youth from ordained minister to coal miner in Kentucky and miner in the copper mines in Arizona. I gulped when he said he kicked large blue hunks of turquoise out of the way and had no time to select any for keeping. Before lunch I heard more from him about himself than I had heard from James in the two years we had dated before we married. I was relieved to discover that he wasn't afraid to talk, or tell me about himself. He invited me to lunch and we stayed over the time allotted by the conference. "You and I have attended meetings before," he said, "but I did not try to meet you because you were either in discussion with someone or on the dance floor. This time I have the advantage."

We attended the last meeting of the session, but I could see out of the corner of my eye that his attention was not on the speaker. His closeness was disconcerting and exciting, yet comfortable in a way I had not felt for years – if ever. I began to believe there was something to this thing called chemistry.

He invited me to have dinner with him. He said he knew a really good seafood restaurant – he thought I'd like it being a native of Mobile. He came for me at seven and I wondered if after all the earlier conversation he had any topics left. He asked a lot of questions in the manner of a man really interested in getting to know another. What kind of music did I like, what kind of art. We found we had much in common. He had been spending time after retiring remodeling old houses and cars. He said, "When you tackle old houses you better know plumbing, carpentering and painting. I was raised on a farm where you have to learn to do everything to make it work."

I told him I had bought three small repossessed houses and designed the remodeling but let others do the work. I had just finished another, the one I was living in at the moment – a 1922 bungalow that the carpenter said "was a new house we built inside an old one." There was too much to tell about it, but I did tell him the story of the glassed-in front porch. I wanted it framed in black wrought iron with a matching door.

I remembered a favorite design on an old house on Government Street with wrought iron hearts repeated in the design. So I had a heart decorated wrought ironwork on the front of my 1922 bungalow, fitting, I thought for an entryway to my group room in my home office. "I have to see that," he said.

We met for breakfast on the last day of the conference. He showed me a brochure announcing the next psychiatric workshop. "I hope you can plan on that one." Soon after I arrived back in Wichita Falls I received a Southwest Airlines plane schedule to his home area in Texas. I read it and knew I was ready to follow him anywhere he might lead.

In the following years we went together to meetings and took vacations together in Mexico, Canada, and my favorites, Arizona and New Mexico. We both had to continue working until retirement, his second at Vernon State Hospital, which would end in 1991. I still had a year to go at that time.

I ended my eighth year of practice in Wichita Falls with a three-year sabbatical in Fairhope. Then Bill, who had moved to Vernon to work in the Maximum Security Hospital there arranged for me to apply for a job with the Adolescent Unit to work as a family therapist with court adjudicated adolescents and their families in the juvenile hospital setting. We bought a house close to the hospital and worked there for seven years.

Sherds – a Mémoire

Bill finished before me. I had one year to go at the time he received a call from Kentucky that both of his sisters were ill and needed help. I told him to go on and I would join him there in a year.

The next year on the day my ten-year retirement was up with the State of Texas, which included three years spent at other State hospitals; Bill came for me in a big SUV pulling a U-Haul. It was great fun driving in the snow all the way to Kentucky. I drove most of the way.

It took only a few weeks to find the house, a stately 30-year-old red brick, white columned house with a colonial flavor in a small cul-de-sac. We enjoyed life there. There was a large yard with trees and shrubs offering opportunities for relaxation and gardening. Bill always found something in the house to repair or improve on. In his spare time he liked to draw. I told him he should be a cartoonist, with his sense of humor and art, a perfect fit.

One Halloween we were invited to a costume party. I asked him to paint a black cat on my long orange skirt. He found some black material, cut out a large figure and sewed the cat from waist to the hem in the style of the long thin Yei figures of the Navajo which he had seen on a skirt I had bought in Arizona.

Another time at Halloween I asked if he could make some kind of scarecrow to place in front of the house. He brought some straw from a nearby field, made a wooden form, dressed it in one of my gingham dresses with a denim apron, put one of my big straw hats on it and painted a good likeness of my face on the life sized scarecrow. Cars stopped abruptly and often in front of the house in what seemed like a parade.

I have had relationships with a number of men through the years, and I usually characterized them with one word. With Bill I had to use at least two: loving and interesting. He spiced up every day situations with some clever surprise. I always anticipated his arrival home with a feeling of excitement. I never spent a bored moment with him, and I never spent any time with him without some expression of affection. He was as methodical and orderly as he was a clever artist. I, on the other hand, had to learn and practice to be orderly, as I was scattered and messy. Happily, he didn't seem to mind.

After a few years he drove himself to "do what was needed." I worried when I saw him pushing himself, even though he was tired. His hobbies had become a drill. In my family we would say, "It can wait until tomorrow" and "take your time." I would have to interrupt his work in the yard with a drink or a cookie to try to make him stop and rest. He would kiss me and thank me and put them aside until he finished the task. I tried to talk him into taking short cuts or using a more efficient tool. He admitted, "I do things the hard way."

As so many men who feel the slowing signs of age, he drove himself more. He had worked all his life, he didn't know how to slow down. During this time he became more pessimistic, more negative. When I would comment on this, he would say, smiling a little, "I'm not pessimistic just realistic." He said I looked at the world through rose-colored glasses, but then he would add, "it's a good thing one of us does." He would say, "you know I'm even tempered, always angry." He never lost his sense of humor or his generous nature. I never had to ask him for anything. He said I was the only one who never did. He said I was the best thing that had ever happened to him. I read this in a Somerset Maugham novel: She was "my reward." Bill was mine.

When he was 75 he suffered a stroke. We were preparing to leave for his church, and he was trying to program the remote for later time in the day. I saw him fumbling with the remote for several minutes, "Honey I can't do it." I was alarmed. He had performed this same task for years. No machine had ever bested him. "Put it down, please," I said. "We're not going anywhere." He lay down on the sofa and I watched him closely. Then, with great effort he said, "I can't talk," I immediately called our physician who said he would meet us at the hospital in 10 minutes. The diagnosis was indeed a stroke. The doctor said, "With a few months of speech therapy he would regain his speech, even though there might be a slight glitch." I felt weak. I knew my perfectionist Bill would not take that news well. He was knowledgeable about stroke and its typical outcomes. He had worked intensively on the medical ward. I had heard him speak about so many patients who failed to regain speech and became blind. I was sure he would think of that. I was actually relieved and optimistic because the stroke was treated swiftly, which I knew was important in recovery.

Bill showed no signs that he did not share my feelings. In the hospital he was active, moving about, even showing concern for me. When mealtime came he motioned that he wanted to share the meals with me. Seeing this was almost too much to bear.

Bill was sent home the next day. He insisted on walking downstairs when I was ready to bring his dinner up to the bedroom. In fact there was another bedroom downstairs, but he refused to use that one. He walked and motioned for me to see how well he could walk. My optimism and good feelings at being able to help him with the speech therapy, in which I had some training, blinded me to the possibility that he would attempt suicide.

In my work I had been quick to predict and prevent suicide in my clients. They always told me or acted out in some bizarre or obvious ways. I was always able to intervene and alert the staff. My positive attitude and urgent desire to help Bill must have shut out even the thought that he did not feel the same way.

I suppose that after the psychologist examined him and proposed a more extensive therapy program than the doctor alluded to, he must have lost hope for a good recovery and decided to give up the struggle and settle for 75 years. I on the other hand, after hearing the psychologist's report, was ready to immediately start helping with the work on the speech therapy and felt certain of success.

Four days from the event of the stroke on Sunday at one o'clock in the morning, he left the bed where I was sleeping and killed himself. I woke up - it was about an hour later, according to the coroner, and found him. I was shocked to see he had hanged himself. I tried to revive him, but it was useless.

There was a wake and a funeral. I was like a sleepwalker through it all as family members took charge of everything.

The only note found on the otherwise empty desktop was on the bottom of a one-page theatre program of a play we had planned to attend. He signed it the way he signed all of his notes and letters to me, ILY.

Butterfly in Black

He circled my head three times around
then thrice my waist, then close to ground
thrice circling the Lilac then the Rose
our favorites were the ones he chose.

It seemed he came to grieve with me
before he sought our favorite tree.
Now you may say it was my scent
that summoned him the way he went

And some would say coincidence
the only call for making sense
and I of course don't know but I
welcomed that errant butterfly.

To Sarah

I lost my Love too late I thought
to have the time to heal my heart
I cried to Heaven "Unfair! Unfair!"
leaving me helpless to prepare
for fragile, weakening older years
no time to learn to cover tears
to compensate for all unsaid
to learn to rest alone in bed

nor learn to cook for only me
or shop for things he'd never see
to seek to wander to explore
beyond a closed protecting door
no time to learn to share again
for oddly strangers heighten pain
the reach for others easy when
my Love was waiting hearthside then.

And then I met another who
excelled at all I couldn't do
the words I found so hard to say
she could in a lighthearted way.

I learned she was a widow too
but lost her love at forty-two
and I was so amazed to find
her grief was still as new as mine.

Losing our loves both soon and late
she seemed the more unfortunate
sharing her loss I wonder how
my blessings were not known till now.

One More Antique

One more antique to fit that wall
perhaps a picture, then that's all.
for every treasure tells a tale
so one excursion, one more sale.

The sight of whimsy, sport or glee
helps hone the craft of memory
so needed now, yet proving dim
of all but memory of him.

And then I'm sure I'll have enough,
for more than needed turns to "stuff."
but empty space seems filled with pain
of scenes I fear to see again.

The glassware sparkling in the sun
can warm me, even spur me on
to polish, sweep and tend the house
as when I did for love of spouse.

Who now no longer chides "that thing?"
and secretly loved all I'd bring,
who smiled his pride when I could say
what little sum was spent that day.

Just one more trip to strain and find
the right antique to calm my mind
so one more day I'll wake and see
fit emblem of his memory.

Priorities

A button came off
and I am out of cornbread
and the kitchen floor has another
chocolate spot
and it's time to take my heart pill
and it's washday
and if I'm to keep my Fica in this weather
I must water it
and the Pittisporum and cover the Gardenias
and bake the cookies for Church
since no one else signed up
and take my dog
who was my companion through the evacuation
of the hurricane
and barked so furiously
at the intruder that he went away
and who when another dog, little dog
bares his teeth and lunges at him
merely stares and considers the source
and after seven years of eating the same dry dog food
comes running every dinner time wagging his tail
and sits patiently
for me when I keep him waiting, which
I labored as a psychotherapist
very hard to teach my clients to do,

so I must take him for his walk
instead of revising retyping rewriting
the dozens of poems and stories
reviewing my life.
And so another day my Mémoire won't be finished.

Bed Making

Bed making used to be a cheerful chore
pink flowers nodding on the sheets in flight
the quilt its story told anew each day
the pillow's dent recalling he was there.

But now bed making is unwanted task
reminding only that I'll sleep alone
but still the pillow soothes and quilt still warms
and I will have his socks for my cold feet.

Brain Exercises

Some write for money
some publish for fame
I write to be able
to write the same

Some choose hard puzzles
to test the brain
I write poems
for mental gain

Their work seems tedious
rewards hard won
my work is fun fun fun
all the day long

Thoughts on a Reading

I relished my rich strong coffee and homemade bread
imbibed the allure of daily mundane things,
I walked and felt the sands as I do every day
and breathed the breeze into my embracing lungs,
then felt inspired to action.

I heard the Mormon Tabernacle Choir's "Impossible Dream"
and believed once more the triumph of hard life.
and then as if by perverse contrast driven
I thought of a great heroine, well drawn well written,
who struggled young and changed herself into a woman
spiting the malefactors and ill fortune –
a new Jane Eyre even in these times,
but by the happenstance of a cleverly written story
forbidden the triumph that accrues with life outwitting death.

And then my dream of triumph is repealed,
my old redundant sadness now returns
and blights the remaining day, retrieving all rewards.
And my William dies again.

Chapter 18 – Starting Over – Again

At age 79 after Bill died I felt the need to move again. Surely I have had enough practice. During the 1940s I used to say the only thing I was expert in was moving. A friend once remarked, "You know how to take leave and make a place for yourself."

Downsizing in the Kentucky home included two auctions and deciding what to take to the condominium on Mobile Bay in Fairhope that Bill and I had purchased three years before for a retirement home. Cutting down the large household was surprisingly easy. Where I was going there would be no dining room, no second living room, no extra bedrooms, no screen porch, no large yard. So the furnishings were not needed in the two bedroom townhouse.

The first year of my marriage James and I moved from town to town eight times, setting up housekeeping from three weeks to at most a month. We moved in the one car carrying only two typewriters, a featherweight sewing machine, my mother's silverware, a skillet, four pans, and a coffee pot. When we were lucky enough to rent a one-bedroom apartment we used suitcases in graduating sizes for a chest of drawers for our clothes. We never thought of these times as hardships, after all it was wartime and everyone was on rationing of all kinds.

During the war years and after my first divorce from James, I worked for four oil companies. All the jobs were arranged for me by James who said we needed the money.

During the three years in social work school and two additional years working toward postgraduate accreditation, I worked in Austin, commuted to San Antonio, and lived in Dallas and Houston. When I was young I had the notion that when one retired a life of leisure would be waiting, including extensive travel. Mary and I had planned several times to travel for a season in Europe, visiting the places of her ancestors, but I was never able to go. As it turned out I made a few trips to Mexico, Canada, a day in New York and Washington, D.C. a week in Chicago, and of course the six years of continuous moving in Texas and Oklahoma. After that travel with Bill was all I desired. I always thought of myself as a traveler in fantasy with my clients as they shared the adventures of their minds and their family dramas.

As I faced a new life alone after so many years of companionship I thought of my indebtedness to James and Bill for starting my career. James promoted my first position at the University of Texas in the Department of Geology which provided the incentive to pursue the field of mental health. Bill introduced me to personnel of the Vernon State Hospital offering financial security, which in order of priorities was always second to my concentration on my work with clients. This seemed natural and necessary because emergencies requiring my attention were an everyday occurrence with little time left over for personal concerns.

I cannot forget the indebtedness to Louis De Moll, who in 1959 when I was the Executive Director of the Wichita Mental Health Association, kindly and patiently encouraged and guided me from volunteer status to the professional social worker I wanted to become. He was my supervisor and supporter of the program I developed in the Confederate Home years, and without whom I could not have accomplished the goals there.

As I faced the final move (I hoped!) I felt secure in my identity. So many people feel lost when they lose the most important person in their lives. I was aware of my abilities and my weaknesses and admitted that my strength always came from the love and support of the people I loved and who loved me.

I was thirteen having finished my Junior High year at Barton Academy, and ready to be a freshman at Murphy high School, when I decided to have a traditional life as a wife and mother. I was among the group of neighborhood girls who were sitting on the lawn drinking lemonade and planning out their lives. That would include college, of course. It was one of those adolescent reveries – we had it all planned out.

I saw my mother succeed in her familial role while maintaining her independence, pursuing interests of her choice and not feeling the need to follow the crowd. I expected to be able to do the same. All of the women of our neighborhood, married or widowed, were strong individuals. They had been able boldly to be themselves. Surely their daughters could do as well. "Oh, yes we might have a job if we liked, but we didn't need a career to prove ourselves." It was unanimous.

Although I became fascinated with journalism and the stage I was too protected and spoiled to consider a confining job with deadlines or one night stands.

Three years later in 1936 Miss Mae Eanes was giving one of her spirited inspirational commencement addresses. I listened, dreaming as I sat in one of the bleachers in my blue peau de soie gown (the girls chose dresses as practical measure instead of cap and gown we could not keep or use again). I had played long enough, I had dabbled and taken flight in the arts long enough, now I declared to myself I would be serious, settle down. I was ready to be a student. I would take the advice of the Managing Editor of the "New York Herald Tribune" who spoke to us at the high school journalists' convention in 1935. He startled us with his challenge, "You've already been students of journalism, when you go to college you don't have to major in it, but learn all you can from literature, the sciences and language, and above all travel and learn about other peoples." And I would take the advice of my father who said, " I don't think you will ever have to work, [!] But you must have a good education, you'll need it."

My destination now was Alabama again, only it would be across the Bay from where I started 61 years ago, the small town of Fairhope. My classmates with whom I had maintained connection through letters and visits all those years had moved from Mobile some years before me. They welcomed me now, as did others in the friendly community which offered abundant opportunities for friendship, music, art, and educational and social programs for older people. After years of working for clients yearning for happiness, I would now join the cadre of people learning to find happiness for themselves while facing old age and learning to live alone.

It was the easiest challenge I could imagine. I credit the many friends and good doctors who helped with every venture. This memoir is not the whole story of my life, of course. In spite of some of the most painful parts omitted here and rose colored glasses granted, I have to say I had it easy.

The last big quest was finding a comfortable home in a beautiful setting. Small or grand, I never had a home I didn't cherish. No matter the situation a suitable and fitting home has always been needed for my grounding. Now I hoped for one which might have something of the character or flavor at least, of the one of my childhood in Atlanta; the large red brick bungalow on the high hill, with the poplar trees lining Linwood Avenue; the one in Mobile on Bienville Avenue, three blocks long, with the three screen porches and a balcony, and the never to be forgotten people of the neighborhood; and the one in Austin with the yellow rose covered arch over a double gate in the one acre yard which supported large Mimosa, long leaf Southern pines, a field of Indian Paintbrush and Blue Bonnets, a long fence of Concord grape vines, and a vegetable garden that supplied produce for the whole neighborhood, in back of the grey stucco house with the French windows that opened over wide stone ledges where the birds came every day at breakfast time.

My House

My house says welcome to my guests,
(and all who come are company)
designed for comfort and discourse
and furnished for my friends and me.

My living room unveils my life
in framed mementoes on the walls,
the bedroom's antique quilts spell rest
and refuge from the wintry squalls.

The kitchen is my warming place,
I like to cook when I am cold,
I scrub and clean when I am hurt,
I'm urged to write when I feel bold.

My dog may make himself at home,
in yard or house he ranges free,
he fancies he is guardian
against the fancied threats to me.

But there's one room we both will claim
as favorite for every need –
the warming kitchen promising
solutions for security.

Downsize to What?

My garden's now my living room
where painted trees and flowers bloom
upon the shelves and on the walls
of bedroom kitchen baths and halls
No more the strolls through canopied lanes
I used to make each day to gain
a boost to spirits. It was then
my garden was my verdant friend.

Bluebonnets grace a blue glass cup
a donkey on Frankoma mug
live swans no longer preen and glide
but now ceramic nest inside
my birds no longer come to feed
now perch on shelves instead of trees.

But now I hear them all termed "stuff"
my lace and needlepoint called "fluff"
"Dream catchers catch just dirt and dust."

Should dolls in cabinets at play
be cavalierly thrown away?
and what about my treasured books?
They're not on bookshelves for their looks
for reference and for joy I keep
they come to bed before I sleep

My chests of jewels gold and stone
enliven every garment owned
on golden oak and velvet lined
each one a gift or lucky find
a gift in turn to someone kind

Four closets of old gowns and shoes
to pay their bills I paid my dues
and now they only take some care
and how much fun they are to share!

The golden horse I used to ride
in portraiture remains my pride.
So must they all be out of sight
For bare and ordered house deemed right?

And when my house is sterile space
what visions come to cheer my place?
The mind a moment can devise
but seeing makes the feeling rise
and when I've vowed to simplify
what sights will soothe me when I cry?
what memories can be reborn
when things reflecting them are gone?

Art Show: Vintage Hats and Gloves Circa 1930-1960

We gave a show for the County
A hundred people came
they talked and laughed and viewed the scene
"Delightful," they proclaimed.

It was a gala party
despite a day of rain.
a hundred people had such fun
that made it worth the game.

We gave a show for the County
a hundred people came
if one saw our intention
that made it worth the game.

On Envying The Artist At Her Show

The human form I cannot sculpt
nor paint nor throw a pot
but I can draw my eyebrows
exactly where they're not

nor shadowed scenes of classics
so prized by connoisseur
but I can shadow my green eyes
and fancy they are bluer

The hair of Titian golden red
beloved down through the ages
is mine for cash at hair salons
in several bottled stages

The lips of pastel maidens
retain their radiant glow
but I with lipstick can restore
my rosy cupid's bow

I cannot cut the patterns
for haute couture designs
but from the village thrift shops
I bring home vintage finds

So if an artist you can't be
nor garner fame or pelf
you can divine a way to be
the artist of yourself

Shower Room Things

I enter my shower room and see
a curly lavender-haired pink-clad dolly
on a tan chintz garden swing
and I smile.
A nearby wall shelf holds a purple swan,
a duck with polka dotted hat
as natural as you please, a tinted Arca wrested
from high tide at Galveston.

My eye can't help but wander fondly
to the 1930 crystalline green dolphin stick
a replica of circa 1830
which rests for some years on the marble counter
suitably beneath the bonneted mermaid whose tucked gown
fabricated from a swirley shell
sashays close to the green glass Santa boot
where matches hide.

Sherds – a Mémoire

Some have said, "How heavy are your walls with stuff!"
But in these somber times
are these purveyors of levity
these quaint provocateurs of smiles
to be expelled?

Nature's Gift

A neighbor brings me roses from her garden
nature's art to compliment my paintings.
A day or two and they have lost their moisture
leaving their color in a wrinkled state,
a fitting compliment to my condition.

Exercise for the Elderly

Think before you-----------fill in the blank

They say that when senility
comes creeping to the door
your erstwhile perspicaciousness
is not as was before.

We're counseled ad nauseum
the likelihood for falls
leaving you to lie in misery
until some neighbor calls.

It's common to get careless
and leave the burner on

and set the house ablazing
from the kitchen to the lawn.

But now I am on top of these
because I still can think
about the stupid acts that
used to bring me to the brink.

When I go for walks now
I am watching every step
I used to never see my feet
Being taught it wasn't hip

When the soup is finished cooking
I remove it from all harm
onto an antique trivet
keeping it chic and safe and warm.

When I drive around a curb
I observe respectful distance
because I've learned my axle
never offers curb resistance.

When I'm working in the kitchen
and in the midst of things
I've learned to sense the danger
when the phone or doorbell rings

because there's no insurance
for a lapse of memory
when any interruption
turns me into my old me.

Career Trilogy

Pride Of The Paleontologist

My fossils garnered no headlines
nor dug an oil well
but my student John made President
of Houston Texas's Shell.

Anatomy Of A Psychotherapist: Tools Of The Trade

My eye has a memory
my ear has a brain
my heart boasts a remedy
for every pain.

Opportunity Forgone: Vertigo

I could have sung at Carnegie Hall
but for the likelihood of a slip
but for a stumble or a sway
but for the chance I'd fall away
at Carnegie Hall

A November Tale

(Spell it how you will)

In November, the autumnal month of fealty to family feasts,
sacrificial feeding of the hungry and homeless, the birth
month of my conservative Father (who nevertheless on
occasion was known to play at poker and bet the horses
in New Orleans), I make confession.
I went to that city of lawlessness,
that den of ultimate thievery,
which my state, that guardian of morality,
that guarantor of virtue
will not allow to sully its farthermost portals,
even there I went for therapeutic respite

For needed relaxation,
for resting my arthritic knees,
to win money.

My withdrawn modicum of hard earned savings
I gleefully fed to that hounding, pounding,
hungry, glowing, gleaming, glassy-eyed monster
seductive calliope machine
two quarters at a time
from time to time now remarkably ahead,
Now suddenly behind.

Finally, with the dedication of an Alabamian,
the discipline of a Puritan,
the rightousness of a Republican,
the devotion of a Democrat
I struggled, wresting away my prize.

I walked guilt free, head high
smiling easily, no, generously
at the oncoming line of aspirants,
fully vindicated for my transgressions
against my State.

Because neither it nor my Social Security
provides for my offspring.

I gratefully re-deposited my retrieval
with my veterinarian
in exchange for services rendered
to the tick-bitten tail
of my faithful Laddie

Thank You Note

I love the early morning
it's when I write the letters
and hear the morning news
and plan the daily schedule
and put it on the calendar
with notes to phone my friends
and set out the ingredients
for baking in the oven
and pay the bills come due.
I still send cards with sentiments
and pictures of my dog.
I love the early morning
it's when I realize
I belong to another century
and appreciate my friends
accepting me in theirs.

Prophesy

Purple splotches midst the beige
taunting prophesy of age
dainty hands and feet no more
plodding to that slippery shore

Waistlines are the first to go
ankles follow fast below

brows and lashes call for dye
leaving eyes to blur and cry

but see the day sure to arrive
determined spirit will survive

Chapter 19 – Milestones

"You can't be Snow White because you're too blonde and too tall – and besides the witch is a much better part."
- My first grade teacher's remarks in answer to my request to audition for the part of Snow White in the class play 1925.

"That is not a real diamond, I told you to buy something good with the dime I gave you."
- My Mother's answer to my displaying for her the ring I bought at Woolworths 5 and 10 cent store in 1928 when I was 9 years old.

"Daughter, you have what is known as a sweet parlor voice,"
- My Father in response to my asking what he thought of my singing in a class recital.

"Moses was a brilliant man, he knew just where to strike the rock to obtain the water."
- My Father in a discussion about miracles in the Old Testament.

"I'm drilling you every day on these food groups, because I want you to always remember these are the ones offering good nutrition: milk and eggs, green leafy vegetables, carbohydrates like corn and rice, and also meat, protein and vitamins."
- My fourth grade teacher beating the drum for good nutrition as she prepared to receive the lunch trays in Highland School in Atlanta, 1929.

"If you will come to Texas I'll give you a pony."
- My Mother's brother, Uncle Frank's promise to me every time he would visit us during my childhood.

"This is a pin put on this new dress by some Paris designer named Chanel. You know I don't wear ornaments – here, you may play with it."

- My Mother's answer to my question when I was playing with my Jacks on the floor, and stopped to see what "the beautiful sparkley thing" was she had removed from the dress she had purchased from Davison Paxon's Department Store in Atlanta.

The photographer was shocked at Mama's 1919 innovative design for a 6 months old.

"Now on the day of your confirmation in the Temple you will read from your selection of the woman, Ruth, of the Old Testament you have chosen to represent you, reading in English, while I read from the Torah."

- The Rabbi of Temple Beth Israel when I told him my choice was Ruth, the Moabite.

"You're not observant, Daughter."

- My Father's comment before he learned I was very near-sighted and needed corrective lenses.

"I won't pay anyone who works for me less than a living wage."

- My Father's answer to a neighbor who complained that he was paying our maid more than the amount the neighbors were paying their servants.

"She's the one, it's her voice, the emotion."

- Ruth Knudson (Groom), Drama coach after hearing me read for the part of the mad woman in Eugene O'Neill's one act play "Ile" at Murphy High School in 1935.

"Mr. Wilson said he would be glad to change the grade on your English theme to an "A" – he just wanted to get a rise out of you."
- My Father reporting on his visit to my 11th grade English teacher after I complained of his unfair treatment to me in his class.

"You don't have to put on the dumb blonde act with me, Jule."
- A brilliant fellow graduate geology student in response to my shyness around him.

"You failed the physical exam prerequisite to being inducted into the WAVES. Try the Red Cross's new program for nurse's aides."
- The Ensign's answer to my question why I failed to get in the WAVES in 1942.

"I'm sweeping your kitchen floor and making you breakfast."
- My brother Frank's answer to my asking him what in the world he is doing up so early after riding the bus all night from the Air Base in North Carolina to visit me in Texas?

"You know your Brother loves you."
- My Father responding to my complaining to him about my Brother Lee's angry remarks to me.

"I fear you are too ambitious."
- The professor of the 17th Century lyric course commenting in red pencil on the play I submitted using the poetic language and style of the 17th century lyric instead of writing a narrative in the usual mode.

"Your handwriting cost me extra time. You must apologize in rhyme."
- My professor of early American prose and poetry teasing me after reading my first theme assignment for his class.

"Are you telling me that you're passing up an opportunity offered you by Dr. Twenhofel to have your condensed version of your thesis published in the Journal of Sedimentology?"

- The question by the Chairman of the Geology Department at the University of Texas to my statement that I didn't have time to re-write, because I was just married and moving the next week to my husband's job location in Oklahoma and I needed to spend my time learning to cook, clean house and sew, none of which I knew how to do.

"You are too practical."

- The Dean of the College of "Arts and Science" at the University of Texas in refusing my request for combining Folklore of the Southwest with Anthropology and Archeology of the Southwest as the subject proposal for my dissertation in literature.

"I came here to kill you because you reported to the Dean my not attending your class, and this caused trouble with my wife, because she did not know I was with my girl friend."

- My paleontology student's answer to my query as to how I could help him when he came to my office one evening.

"You have brought cosmos out of chaos, and I am offering you a continuing position as instructor of invertebrate paleontology at the University of Texas with tenure."

- The chairman of the Department of Geology in a letter to me after receiving my letter of thanks and resignation of my temporary two year position because of my need to accompany my husband who had completed his Ph.D. program and had chosen a position with the Humble Company in Houston.

"Well, Jule, it took me and three other accountants from out of town to arrive at the income tax on your stock transactions. But we came up with the total you had guessed at last week, $2000.00."

- My tax accountant's response to my day trading in the stock market in 1969.

"The stock market – it's a game."
- One of the important lessons my Mother taught me about the stock market.

"But Mrs. Moon, you're a geologist, look at this file again and tell me why my oil wells are going dry."
- The response of the CEO of his company to my statement that the file folder he had just handed me had a brief letter about the climate and cost operations for the month on one well and no other information, and besides I was not an oil field geologist.

"Mrs. Moon , you don't have to say "good morning" when answering the switchboard, "good morning" is unnecessary,"
- The President of the Oil Company when he overheard my answering a call on the switchboard, which was one of my duties as receptionist.

"I'm not interested in all that. I want you to be my chief social worker. Name your price."
- The impatient retort of the Psychiatrist, Chief of the Cornell University Medical School Outpatient Clinic at our first meeting on his visit to our hospital, after I protested that I had not finished out the year in my first hospital job and felt I was not qualified to accept his offer.

"All right, the procedure I'm ordering for this patient is that you'll do the sodium amytal interview without the sodium amytal."
- My psychoanalyst supervisor at the San Antonio Hospital Outpatient Clinic in response to my refusal to use the sodium amytal injection because I was a social worker and not qualified to employ medicine in treatment.

"You broke the rule! You broke the rule of the identity exercise by picking a "beautiful white bird" instead of a lowly scavenger as directed by the leader!"
- The accusation of a member of the professional workshop on the subject of identity in Aruba in 1975, in which we were instructed to select a scavenger as our alter ego and I selected the Snowy Egret.

"I want a Jule Moon."
- A psychiatrist colleague of my associate, alluding to his decision to offer our type of family group therapy in his practice and was looking for an assistant to be in charge of the group.

"Will the little lady from Texas come up to the stage and present us with a style show before we begin the program?"
- The chairman of ceremonies in charge of an international symposium of psychiatric experts on mental health at Bethesda, Maryland 1960 after seeing my hand-painted dress depicting the new mental health center in Wichita Falls, Texas where I was executive director.

"Mrs. Moon, you understand us because you're like one of us."
- A patient, during a therapy session at the San Antonio State Hospital Outpatient Clinic.

"I want you to tell my fortune."
- Virginia Satir, internationally known family therapist and pioneer in the field, during her large workshop group program in which members were instructed to express to the group something they had done which was "the most fun" and I said mine was taking a course in fortune telling from a University of Texas parapsychologist.

"I told you 20 years ago when I first met you that you should be a fortune teller, and I say it now and offer you a chance to learn my method which was taught to me by a nun when I was a child in the convent. We'll arrange for you to try it out on strangers for practice, and at the end of the class you'll be given a certificate. All right, your two friends with you can also attend the classes."

- The invitations extended to me on my second visit after 20 years to a famous parapsychologist.

"Your enthusiasm."
- Statement by Louis De Moll, Chief Social Worker at Texas State Mental Health and Mental Retardation Department. In answer to my question, "What qualities do I have that lead you to think I should go into social work?"

"Now the Director doesn't want any trouble, now he wants you to take over a new and better position in Austin evaluating patients for nursing homes."
- The administrative assistant to the director of a project involving all the Texas State Mental Hospitals for their Department of Research, immediately after my being fired by the Director upon completing the project which he and 5 other Department Heads had signed, when I replied that I would call Senator John Tower and make a report of his firing me.

"Mrs. Moon, I tried what you suggested, taking a vacation together and making compromises, but I say this: I would rather just go to work, do my job, go home and take a pill, and eat supper and go to sleep by myself than continuing in therapy."
- A patient's decision about her conflict: staying in her marriage or leaving her husband.

"I won't let anyone get you, I want you for myself."
- My Bill on our first date, responding to my anxiety while walking late at night on a dark street in San Antonio after dining at a secluded restaurant.

"You are 53, an ideal age for a facelift, with good skin and cheekbones. You will have a problem with vision in later life without it. Have the surgery, I can tell you this will be fun."
- Dr. Dunton, my plastic surgeon in answer to my questions about the advisability for a facelift.

Addendum

(Some of the best Advice I have received before the age of 50)

Love mercy, do justly, and walk humbly with thy God.
- Micah the Old Testament

Seek beauty, give service, pursue knowledge, be trustworthy, hold on to health, glorify work, be happy.
- The Campfire Girls' Creed.

Do unto others as you would have them do unto you.
- The Golden Rule

Know thyself, do nothing too much.
- Inscription on the Temple at Delphi

To thine own self be true. Thou canst not then be false to any man.
- William Shakespeare

Faith, hope, and charity, and the greatest of these is charity.
- Paul of Tarsus

Turn again, Dick Whittington, Lord Mayor of London.
- Mother Goose

A humble life with peace is better than a splendid one with danger and risk.
- The country mouse to the town mouse - Aesops Fables.

For it is love alone that rules for aye.
- Victor Herbert

All the news that's fit to print.
- The New York Times

Accuracy, terseness, accuracy.

- The New York Herald Tribune

Sweet are the uses of adversity.
- William Shakespeare

Worth makes the man and want of it the fellow
The rest is all but leather and prunella.
- Alexander Pope

If you do it unto the least of these you do it also unto me.
- Jesus of Nazareth

Never borrow without being able to cover with collateral.
- My Father

When you gamble on anything always consider the risk.
- My Mother

The opposite of love is fear.
- Psychological precept.

Avoid clichés like the plague.
- My journalism teacher.

He praycth well who loveth well, both man and bird and beast.
- Samuel Taylor Coleridge

A person must love his work.
- My Father

Live in a house by the side of a road and be a friend to man.
- Sam Walter Foss.

Don't let the sun go down on your anger.
- Ephesians 4:20-27

A person must live within her means.
- My Mother

When you are being criticized be sure to consider the source and their needs.
- Precept of psychotherapy.

Whatever befalls the earth befalls the children of the earth.
- Chief Seattle

It pays to advertise.
- Author unknown

Listen to yourself.
- Virginia Satir

Don't be a sheep.
- Jule Moon

Epilogue

The Lesson

I went to the sea to study life
and found the curriculum weighted in loss
now Memory asks, "Did you pass my test?"
and I reply, "I'm here."

About the Author

Figure 1 - Laddie, 2010

Jule Jacobson Moon, a native of Atlanta, Georgia, spent her teenage years active in music, dramatics, and journalism in Mobile, Alabama during the 1930s.

After receiving a Master's Degree in Geology at the University of Texas and teaching paleontology there to World War II veterans, she saw the need for the development of community mental health centers.

After acquiring a Master's Degree in Social Work she chose multiple family therapy as the most effective and economical resource for troubled families. She developed multiple family therapy programs in several Texas mental health clinics and Texas State Hospitals, as well as private practice.

With her dog, Laddie, she makes her home in Fairhope, Alabama where she continues her lifelong involvement in music and writing.

Ten percent of the proceeds from this book will go to The Haven.

Support your local animal rescue center and animal shelter. – Jule